the trustafarian

Handbook

8/10

$350 salon-styled dreads

$8.95 organic açai berry smoothie

$195 brand-name cashmere baja

$∞ Mom and Dad's credit card

$1,275 weekend getaway

$100 pocket change *(he will not bend down to get)*

A Field Guide to the **Neo-Hippie Lifestyle** Funded by Mom and Dad

Brian Griffin

Adamsmedia
Avon, Massachusetts

Published by
Adams Media, a division of F+W Media, Inc.
57 Littlefield Street, Avon, MA 02322. U.S.A.
www.adamsmedia.com

ISBN 10: 1-4405-0215-3
ISBN 13: 978-1-4405-0215-6
eISBN 10: 1-4405-0730-9
eISBN 13: 978-1-4405-0730-4

Printed in the United States of America.

10 9 8 7 6 5 4 3 2 1

Library of Congress Cataloging-in-Publication Data
is available from the publisher.

This publication is designed to provide accurate and authoritative information with regard to the subject matter covered. It is sold with the understanding that the publisher is not engaged in rendering legal, accounting, or other professional advice. If legal advice or other expert assistance is required, the services of a competent professional person should be sought.

—From a *Declaration of Principles* jointly adopted by a Committee of the American Bar Association and a Committee of Publishers and Associations

Many of the designations used by manufacturers and sellers to distinguish their product are claimed as trademarks. Where those designations appear in this book and Adams Media was aware of a trademark claim, the designations have been printed with initial capital letters.

Illustrations by Daniel Hanafin
Interior photos: frisbee © istockphoto/LisaValder, hacky sack © istockphoto/
Ezekiel11, money © istockphoto/ktsimage, passport © istockphoto/davincidig,
home bar © istockphoto/OlsenMatt; all other images © 123RF

This book is available at quantity discounts for bulk purchases.
For information, please call 1–800–289–0963.

For Mom and Dad,
who can read this with pride every time they buy a copy

Contents

Introduction

You would too, if you had the green.

Trustafarians . . .

They are the unsung shaping force of the White Economy, with the power to single-handedly turn billionaire breadwinners into muddled millionaires, taking from the rich and giving to whomever. They inhabit the largest studio apartments in the least affordable neighborhoods, though they are never quite sure how they got there. They call Mom once a week on their smart phones, but only at key times when they are sure she will not answer. Their staccato messages to her lack any notable salutations and end quickly after requests for funding.

For many of this social master class, it is important to note the comma between "filthy" and "rich." Dreadlocked hair is often only washed when they go to the salon to have more wax applied. Even then, the cleaning is a mostly futile effort, but they have both the time and the money to let someone else try. It is a life of leisure for a young Caucasian, and a life that just might be guided by a casual subscription to an Afrocentric religion.

Of course, not all Trustafarians spend their days spinning a second-hand Marley LP on the retro-style turntable they picked up at Brookstone. Not all Trustafarians mold their unkempt hair into dreads, and not all of them use their religion to justify their weed—which they all do use or, at least, say that they use. Some have hair that is completely without style, and many do not have religion at all. They do, however, all have the means to be the rich, watch-wearing jackasses that are more comfortably loathed, but instead, they hide among their lower-net-worth peers.

If you are mildly observant and use the tips given by this handbook, you will be able to spot them with ease.

Why Are They So Fascinating?

There are only a few reasons you bought or "borrowed" this book:

- You are a Trustafarian who does not realize that he/she is supposed to be dreadfully lacking in self-awareness, and you want to find out more about your own culture.
- You are the parent of a Trustafarian and wondering what your child really does with his/her time and your money.
- You have never heard of Trustafarians. This is because you probably work a lot in a small town without any college campuses—either that or you are too busy flying off to your island in Dubai to see what your progeny are up to.
- You are very wise and have an unbridled jealousy for these people, who have won *The Game of Life* decades before you ever will. With no authority figures, dozens of ironic philosophies, hundreds of ways to hate you, and an arsenal of beleaguered but capable lawyers on standby, the Trustafarians have nothing to fear except being cut off—but in truth, if Mommy and Daddy let them get this far, there exists little foreseeable end to the funding.

Many regular folks have had brief encounters with Trustafarians, though they may not have realized it. When Trustafarians finally build up enough motivation to leave their apartments, they often do so in the guise of regular, working-class folks that they learned about from watching *Roseanne* reruns on TV Land. Fortunately, the Trustafarians are not the most successful societal chameleons, with a slew of idiosyncrasies that betray them.

You may find them napping, naked behind the counter of boutique stores, which they own and which never seem to be open. You may catch a tangy whiff of them in a community park, where, during the course of a normal workday, they are taking hits from a bong they made from an organically grown pomegranate with a French horn mouthpiece cleverly thrust into its rind. You may spot them in their chauffeured limited edition Range Rovers as their necks crane out the back window to call you "the Man."

Initial reactions will be those of confusion, and then anger. With time, wonder and jealousy follow. Who are these people that are so free and have it all?

Laid out here in the following pages is—finally—a detailed guide to understanding your Trustafarian neighbors and justifying your jealousies because Trustafarians manage to achieve what so few others can in life. Absolutely nothing.

Who would not love to relax and do absolutely nothing?

Trustafarian Profiles
How to Not Mistake a Homeless Person for a Trustafarian

> **trustafarian** (trŭst´tə-fär´ē-ən) n.
> *English*: any member of a social class of dependently wealthy people, generally ages eighteen to forty, who attempt affecting lifestyles that conceal their affluence while still maintaining a life of leisure
> *Trustafarian*: someone else, not me

Much like the Illuminati or the Mafia, the Trustafarians exist as a camouflaged upper crust with the means to attain great power—though unlike the other two well-connected groups, they lack any desire to do so. They are among us, and it is normal to be frightened, excited, or fascinated. Trustafarians can be difficult to spot, often hiding in plain sight, though never before noon or maybe 3:00 P.M.

While they try to blend among hipsters, stoners, and black people, Trustafarians can generally be identified by the discrepancies in their lifestyle. You may be presented with the following puzzles:

- How did that impoverished hippie get a better seat than me on the plane?
- Why is the senator's daughter asleep in that bus shelter?
- How does that out-of-work young man afford that _____?
  (This blank may be filled in with such items as "spacious loft apartment,"

"brand-new BMW," "$8,000 Cavalier King Charles Spaniel mix," or "bangin' hot girlfriend.")

If you find yourself confronted with one or more of these head-scratchers, it is highly likely you have stumbled across a Trustafarian. Of course, you want what they have, but if you find yourself wanting to express any contempt, try to hold back. Remember, they are more spiteful of you than you are of them.

That hostility is one uniting factor among the Trustafarians. Outwardly it will be directed at you, unless you are black or very poor, but if pressed to define the hostility, a Trustafarian will eventually deflect. Whether capitalism, racism, or Bernie Madoff is making him/her sour, the root of the evil can ultimately be traced back to rich white folks like your Trustafarian, who will have exited the conversation by that point.

Adopting Trustafarian culture allows rich white progeny to distance themselves from themselves and adopt new personas that society can dislike for reasons entirely different than "being the Man." For Trustafarians, and indeed for many others, this Man is a loathed embodiment of all oppression, and he could be anyone, male or female. Parents and white-collar workers are first in line for the title, but it may also be applied to an old woman who asks a Trustafarian for help getting something down off a high shelf. (Who is *she* to request that the Trustafarian stops what he/she is doing, just to make her own life a little bit easier?) The Man is the antithesis of any Trustafarian ideal, no matter how temporary.

- Being the Guy who brings bedbugs into nice residential areas
- Being the Dude who violates dress codes, quiet hours, and your precious daughter
- Being the Entrepreneur who does not concern herself with money
- Being the Girl known by name at Jamba Juice
- Being the Fourth in line for the new Apple product
- Being the Seventh-year Senior

If you are worried about being the Man yourself, you will do well to avoid the Trustafarians. Any contrary step on their paths will result in immediate distrust and malice. You will be the Man. After that point, it is difficult to reestablish favor. Still, many people will risk these potential missteps because Trustafarian interactions are truly unique moments. However, if you are at all afraid, watch out for Trustafarians and keep your distance. This handbook will show you what they look like and where to find them. Interact or evade as you will.

There are several options that a trust fund child may choose from when deciding to become a Trustafarian. The following pages will highlight the principal Trustafarian types.

FIGURE 1.a. *prodigofilius rastaphilia*

the
impostafarian

Impostafarian (ĭm-pŏs′tə-fär′ē-ən): a Trustafarian who proclaims Jah provides, while accepting provisions from Mom and Dad; often observed in Prospect Park, looking for a drum circle, and wearing their new dashikis.

Often to the sheer bewilderment of their melanin-strong, assumed brethren, Impostafarians proclaim Haile Selassie to have been the reincarnation of Christ and support the Rastafari movement or as much of it as they can intuit from Bob Marley songs and relevant Wikipedia articles.

One of the first things you will notice (and the last thing they will) is that Impostafarians are not particularly black. There exists a valid argument to be made here that white people were birthed from Africa as well, and many black people do accept other races as being legitimate members of the Rastafari movement. Still, there is strong sentiment among many members of all races that this melding is just too weird. Because an Impostafarian may fear being pummeled, he/she may choose to practice his/her Rastafarian beliefs in private, or at least tone them down in front of real black people.

- **LIKELY COLLEGE MAJORS:** African Studies; Afro-American Studies; African Languages and Lit.; Dropping out and watching reruns of *A Different World*

- **LARGEST EXPENSES:** Lock of Marley's hair; hospital bills after getting punched (by any number of people); salon visits to touch up the dreads

- **DREAM IN LIFE:** To return to his/her or another someone's Ethiopian motherland

FIGURE 1.b. *prodigofilius sanctimonia*

the
fauxlanthropist

Fauxlanthropist (fō′lăn-thrə-pist): a Trustafarian for whom a typical gait is a protest march, though the reason for the march is generally unclear; often observed distributing flyers in Dolores Park.

Flammable income is seen by these Trustafarians as a means to save the world, one arbitrary cause at a time. Unused portions of their monthly stipends go to fund fundraisers, charity exhibitions, and opening galas. If there is an opportunity to make helping the less fortunate a good time, the Fauxlanthropist will take it. Pabst Blue Ribbon may be the extent of the open bar, but just knowing that their money made it happen is all the satisfaction these Trustafarians need.

Females will typically sport what they consider to be tasteful dreadlocks, often pulled neatly back in an elastic band or even with pieces of their own hair that they have had to cut out. The males generally appear scruffy, but with some Axe body spray and vintage attire, grunge is overlooked. With the right touches these Trustafarians can be presentable when talking to perspective vendors, party planners, minor celebrities, or maybe even a sickly orphan.

- **LIKELY COLLEGE MAJORS:** Art; Gender and Sexuality; Women's Studies; Make-Your-Own-Major

- **LARGEST EXPENSES:** Hybrid car with custom color; $20,000 event that pulled in $700 for charity

- **DREAM IN LIFE:** To be thanked for something really special

FIGURE 1.c. *prodigofilius dudes*

the
brohemian

Brohemian (brō-hē′mē-ən): a member of the most social subset of Trustafar ians, exclusively acting and reacting with a group mentality; often observed on the Amherst College campus years after graduation.

These are the most social of the Trustafarians, keeping their bros close at all times. The name skews to the masculine, but lady Brohemians do exist. Within both sexes of Brohemians there is a strong resistance to change. Cabals are formed in prep school and college, and out of school, the groups remain fixed. The Brohemians are not comfortable forming opinions without the help of their crews.

Though considered the most preppy of Trustafarians, bandanas, flip-flops, and tie-dye often add panache. These are not typically frat boys, and if for some reason they went Greek, it was one of those ugly-duckling frats, where everyone was welcomed and the only six-packs were in the fridge. Similarly, the females have likely never been sorority girls, and if they were, they certainly gave the finger and walked within a semester.

After college, Brohemian Trustafarians find themselves living more of a frat life than ever, often choosing to live in their college towns with their buds, smoking buds.

- **LIKELY COLLEGE MAJORS:** English; History; Economics; Undeclared; What Dad said

- **LARGEST EXPENSES:** Party bus rental; yearlong vacations in Thailand; hush money

- **DREAM IN LIFE:** Road trip around the world with the whole crew, possibly by yacht or helicopter

FIGURE 1.d. *prodigofilius limon*

the
diddlysquatter

Diddlysquatter (dĭd′lē-skwŏt′ər): a Trustafarian whose body and couch have evolved complementary shapes; not often observed in public but may generally be found napping in their East Village studio.

It is the same as when you refer to a busted hatchback: These Trustafarians are lemons. They simply do not work. No amount of prodding is going to change that. Their parents realized this and stopped trying years ago, leaving the Diddlysquatters alone in their secluded and coveted peace. What separates this group from the Fauxlanthropist, the Brohemian, and the Impostafarian is that the Diddlysquatter has zero involvement in the way of charitable endeavors, political agendas, social causes, or anything requiring motivation. Flip-flops, weed, disdain for the Man, resentment toward parents, and lack of self-awareness are very much intact.

- **LIKELY COLLEGE MAJORS:**
  Rarely applicable; Undeclared through drop-out date

- **LARGEST EXPENSES:**
  3,000-square-foot loft apartment in an up-and-coming area; every game console ever; twice-daily pizzas

- **DREAM IN LIFE:** N/A; ask them when they wake up

FIGURE 1.e. *prodigofilius vampirus*

the
heirasite

Heirasite (âr′ə-sīt′): a person with latent or adult-onset Trustafarianism; often observed in Prospect or Dolores Park, on the Amherst campus, or in an East Village loft, getting chummy with other Trustafarian types.

The American Dream has been redefined for the Heirasites. These are the self-made Trustafarians, who prove that anything is possible when you lack personal accomplishments, a basic strategy, and long-term goals of your own. "Anything" in this case is the siphoning of funds from a legitimate Trustafarian. Their uncanny achievement should not be overlooked, as they give hope that even grownups who never smile can find their own Daddy Warbucks. If you are a parent of a Trustafarian (POT), you are probably wondering how such an outrageous thing could happen. If you are not a POT, your mind is racing, wondering, "How can I be an Heirasite!" To achieve Heirasite notoriety, you must meet these three criteria:

- **LIKELY COLLEGE MAJORS:** College is unlikely, but they were voted Class Artist in high school

- **LARGEST EXPENSES:** They do not buy anything themselves; smoothies/frozen coffee drinks

- **DREAM IN LIFE:** That their Trustafarian lives to be 100

STEP 1: You assume the traits of either the Impostafarian, the Fauxlanthropist, the Brohemian, or the Diddlysquatter.

STEP 2: You enter a long-term relationship with a Trustafarian and become inseparable.

STEP 3: Your Trustafarian buys you everything you could ever need and want.

Your Trustparents will never be pleased with your existence, but it does not matter, as the Trustafarian holds the power in this situation. If your Trustafarian is ever faced with choosing between your love and his/her stipends, you will at least be kicked out knowing you lived the dream for a little while.

trustparent (trŭst′pâr′ənt) n.
Heirasite: your Trustafarian's Mom, Dad, and their respective spouses
Other Trustafarians: (not used; the relationship between a friend and a parent is completely irrelevant.)

How to Spot a Trustafarian

The primary modus operandi of a Trustafarian is to blend in with the lower socioeconomic castes. This makes spotting them a challenge, but if you find yourself in a metropolitan or college area and know the right signs, you will be able to pick them out of the crowd!

TRUSTAFARIAN TELLS

Look for these giveaway signals if you think you may have found a Trustafarian:

- Pinky is extended when knocking back a 40 ounce
- Home bar is stocked with top-shelf vodka brands you have never heard of
- Decorations are pictures from his/her semester at sea
- Baja or hemp shirt has that unmistakable off-the-rack smell or tags still on it
- Fender bender is dubbed "totaled" for the purposes of getting new Bentley
- White rich person resents your whiteness/envies your blackness
- They do not seem to mind that they dropped that C-note (You do not either.)
- Hobo is welcomed, not shooed away, by doorman
- He/she is "in between jobs" without having previously worked
- He/she knows when the soup kitchen is serving minestrone and thinks it is almost as good as the kind Nanny used to make
- He/she is playing poorer, blacker version of self on *The Sims 3* iPhone app
- Hair looks worse coming out of salon

FIGURE 1.f. *The home bar*

Before　　　　　　　　**After**

FIGURE 1.g. *Seeing a Trustafarian after getting her hair done may leave you puzzled. Did she exit a salon or a macramé academy?*

A certain delicacy is required to really get to know the Trustafarians. Integration with them is highly unlikely unless you have a substantial monetary backing. The self-made or nouveau riche are seen as unwelcome overachievers. However, if you happen to live below the poverty line or are a Rastafarian, the Trustafarians may just crave integration with *you*.

TRUST FUN! | ## Trust Fund, Trust *Friend*

This is the first of many special Trust Fun sections in this handbook that are painstakingly designed to help you experience the world of Trustafarians beyond these pages.

Befriending a Trustafarian is a unique experience that may be filled with pleasant surprises and unpleasant pitfalls. This handbook will help you learn what to look out for. Here is what to do if you want to make a Trustafarian your friend (the easy way!).

STEP 1: Find a Trustafarian.

STEP 2: Hit him/her with a Hacky Sack or a Frisbee. Say, "My bad!" (Now you have the Trustafarian's attention! Good work!)

FIGURE 1.h. *Attention getters*

STEP 3: When they look like they want to harm you, stop the tension by saying, "You look familiar. Did you go to _____?" Fill in this blank with the name of your nursery school or church, e.g., "St. Paul's." The Trustafarian will wonder if this is a prestigious prep school. Before he/she can question the institution . . .

CONTINUED ON NEXT PAGE

STEP 4: Gripe about how your dad forced you to go. Say how you wish he had just given you the money instead of wasting it there.

STEP 5: If your Trustafarian is willing to take on friends, you are now in the running! Suggest some ganja or drinks without being too creepy about it.

In no time at all, you will be great friends, until your Trustafarian gets bored.

NOTE: If you are dressed in too preppy or professional a manner, try putting a twig in your hair. It will give you that alfresco edge you need to be more likeable.

Tips from the Trustafarian Trenches

Trustafarians are white people. On rare occasion a Trustafarian of Asian decent will arise, but this is astonishingly infrequent and akin to spotting an albino Chinese river dolphin. It is a lucky day for you if you are in that right place at that right time.

Trustafarians live a fragile existence and often carry a lot of stress. Do not piss them off. They could very well call someone to hurt you.

When observing Trustafarians in their natural habitats (which also tend to be the habitats for many unidentified protozoa who shack up there), remember that they do not sleep in alleyways because they have to. It is because they want to and are just too tired to make it the rest of the way home. Be very careful chatting with an alley dweller about their trust fund. It is simply in poor taste.

Spot the Differences!

Are you ready to test what you have learned? Take a look at the following two images and see if you can spot six differences between the Trustafarian and the legitimate vagrant!

Trustafarian	Vagrant

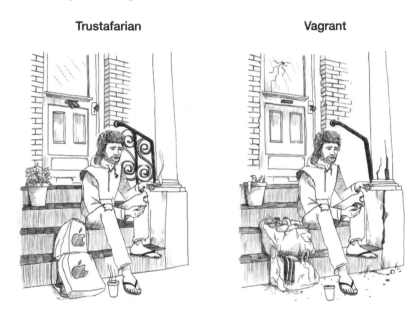

Solution:
1. The Trustafarian is clearly checking his Facebook page. The legitimate vagrant is hungry.
2. The Trustafarian's bags hold impulse buys from the Apple Store. The legitimate vagrant's bags hold most of his belongings.
3. The legitimate vagrant's pants are torn from months of wear and tear. The Trustafarian's pants are torn "ironically" by Urban Outfitters.

4. The legitimate vagrant got his hair cut for free. The Trustafarian paid $175 (with tip).
5. The legitimate vagrant is outside a rundown apartment. The Trustafarian is outside the legitimate vagrant's old apartment he was run out of due to gentrification.
6. The Trustafarian is holding a blunt stuffed with some great weed he scored. The legitimate vagrant is holding the cash he got from selling the Trustafarian an ounce of crushed maple leaves.

How did you do on this challenge? It is not as easy as you thought—is it? Well, do not worry! There are still plenty more things to learn about the Trustafarians in the following chapters.

CHAPTER 2

Pinnacle of Human Success

Retirement at Age Eighteen

You are probably beginning to become jealous of Trustafarians, unless you have as much money and leisure time as they do. And if you do have as much, then you certainly do not have as many years left to enjoy them because you are retired—and death is just a weak-armed stone's throw away. If this is your situation, do not feel that your accomplishments are at all diminished when you finally take that long-dreamed-about bus trip to Everest, only to see a grungy twenty-four-year-old smoking up with a Sherpa at base-camp, while you wait down in the vehicle. You worked hard for that trip, and that Trustafarian will never experience your sense of accomplishment. Take pride in that.

Octogenarians and Trustafarians: More in Common than the Age of Their Hips

Much like the elderly, Trustafarians are confronted with continual ennui. Both groups lack sufficient intellectual stimuli and challenges that require anything more than balance or basic lifting strength.

Most likely you have been told to listen to your elders for the wisdom that they can provide. For those of you still searching for that wisdom, in studying Trustafarians, you finally have an opportunity for the elderly to become relevant! Understanding one group will help you in understanding the other. Often, older Americans and Trustafarians are unaware that they have a sister class. Here is but a sampling of their many similarities.

EXCESSIVE FREE AND ALONE TIME

Why so much time to spare? The elderly have worked hard for upwards of seventy years. They have outlived their spouses and most of their friends. Trustafarians probably worked for seventy seconds before quitting, and their friends are either busy at work or nonexistent. Sleeping only fills so much of the day. The result for both groups is a Sunday *New York Times* puzzle completion time of fourteen minutes, eight seconds.

FIGURE 2.a. *Ink only: a completed crossword puzzle, done in pen, not pencil. Trustafarians and the elderly both live for the moment. There is no going back, and they are sure they can do no wrong.*

IMPAIRED DRIVING

With poor vision, tired eyes, and slower reflexes, the elderly often lack that pep and zing they used to have in their younger days. The Trustafarians are just fried and cannot see that much of the road over their portable Blu-ray player. Both circumstances lead to decelerated reaction times and accelerated bumper-to-bumper kissing. It is not all unpleasant though. Both groups get a brief thrill when they hit something with a motor carriage. Do not question them about this though. They will not admit to vehicular wrongdoing. Remember, potholes are the real menaces on the road (especially when they yelp or get their collars stuck in the grille). Taking a ride with a member of either group in the driver's seat will likely be full of experiences you will need to forget.

SOCIALLY ACCEPTED OLD-PEOPLE CRAZY

Old-People Crazy, or OPC, is a sought-after affectation that usually is achieved somewhere over the metaphorical hill. This collection of quaint and curmudgeonly quirks would be seen as reprehensible in most social groups. The elderly and Trustafarians can get away with OPC because no one is going to stop them.

Both groups can say whatever they want whenever they want. There is no reason to censor themselves, as offending anyone is not a concern, and there is no way to predict what will roll off their unrestrained tongues. Prepare to hear loud complaints about fungal infection at five-star restaurants, retellings of Richard Pryor jokes about race relations, and the casual outing of suspected homosexuals. Any attempt to correct politically incorrect OPC will just result in a blank stare followed by an offensive comment directed at you.

GOLDFISH MEMORIES

Like the elderly, Trustafarians are not responsible for remembering anything. Birthdays can happen at any time, and valuables just tend to get lost or misplaced. Similarly, Trustafarians can tell the same story again and again to the same person. This is allowed because 1) nothing new has happened and he/she has nothing else to talk about, and 2) it is simply not worth explaining that you have already heard the story, because he/she will finish telling it anyway (and often make up some new details).

YOUTH IS WASTED LIKE THE YOUNG

The main difference between these sister groups is time. The Trustafarians have loads of it and the elderly have minutes. This is why the Trustafarians are so successful. What normally takes nearly the entirety of a lifetime is given to them as soon as they complete high school or the attempted parts of higher education. In rare cases, lackadaisical parents will let them achieve this at age sixteen, or whenever a child may legally drop out of school.

Everyone wants funding for leisure time, and the Trustafarians have it. The stars for which they reach are not particularly far off the ground, so with relative ease, they are satisfied and successful. There may be some guilt issues (which will be discussed later) but there is nothing too grave that it cannot be dealt with by swiping a credit card or just telling Mom to take care of it. This is why you should be jealous. This is what you cannot have.

Enjoying the Finer Things in Life

Retirement is about much more than a cool-down run before death. It is a passive-aggressive battle to become the coolest retiree around. Trustafarians are just as competitive as older retirees. A Trustafarian will see others in his/her situation perhaps buying the complete DVD collection of John Waters' films. To compete, without ever admitting it of course, the Trustafarian will get the same DVD collection, snag a producing credit on the *Hairspray* sequel, sprout a Waters-approved teeny, tiny mustache, and gloat privately before losing interest and never unwrapping the DVDs.

TRUSTAFARIAN SPOTLIGHT ON

Patty Hearst

Now Patricia Hearst Shaw, and more of a socialite than a Trustafarian, this heiress, granddaughter of mega-publisher William Randolph Hearst, once made headlines for her kidnapping and subsequent foray into bank robbery. After that episode and a Carter-commuted prison sentence, her Trustafarian leanings drove her to an acting career, and she has now appeared in every John Waters film since *Cry-Baby.*

GLOBE-PLODDING

Travel is a key component of a satisfying leisure life. Staying in the same place for too long just gets depressing, especially for Trustafarians, who never bothered to decorate or have the roof fixed. Travel also gives the Trustafarians something on which to report to parents, who are always asking, whether with actual curiosity or not, what their spawn is up to. The three-month vacations also give Trustafarians an excuse not to talk to their parents for the three months that they are out of the country, and as a bonus, many other Trustafarians will be jealous.

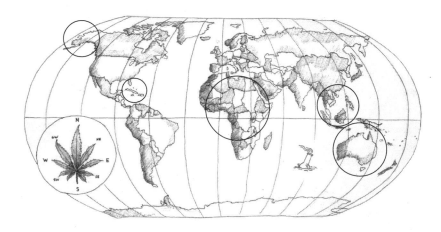

FIGURE 2.b. *If you are having trouble running into Trustafarians around town, try these global Trustafarian hot spots!*

Thailand and Other Eastbound Destinations

In Thailand, the U.S. dollar fares pretty well, which means when Trustafarians hit up their parents for $4,800, it will go much further than in many popular international tourist destinations. There are also beautiful beaches and promises of getting laid (which often involves spending the relatively well-faring U.S. dollar). And, of course, there is Thai food, which is the most frequently used Trustafarian take-out menu after pizza. Clearly the country birthing that food must be the place to be.

An American in Thailand, who is only there for reasons of (sex) tourism, is only allowed to stay for thirty days. After thirty days, that border must be crossed, and Asia offers many other places for Trustafarian travel.

Cambodia is often considered a choice destination for weed-smokers, even though the "happy pizzas" have been banned from menus. Despite the crackdown, it maintains its relaxed reputation. Nepal offers a chance to hunt the Yeti. Bali is a choice destination for those Trustafarians fascinated with Bollywood films, but ultimately confused by portmanteaus.

FIGURE 2.c. *"Getting one's passport stamped" is a very popular euphemism.*

High Seas

Many young people today misinterpret cruising as something that is exclusive to either old folks or lecherous congressmen. Cruising is really for any rich people who like to have fun. Poorer folks stay in hotels and walk to various destinations. Cruisers float their hotels right to where they want to go, and there are lobster tails on the buffet!

It seems like a perfect situation, but there is one sore spot for many Trustafarians, and also for many reasonable people of all classes. It is exceptionally difficult and stressful to bring along some herb to enjoy on what should be a relaxing getaway. The gangplank is not too difficult to ascend undetected, but there are generally airports and customs involved. When visiting other countries, marijuana can generally be purchased, but not knowing where to go can stymie a traveler. Unfortunately, the selection in the luxury ship's gift shop is hopelessly limited.

TAPING CONTRABAND VEGETATION TO YOUR SACK: A TRUSTAFARIAN BELEAGUERMENT

Trustafarians who look like Trustafarians—in other words, the ones whose hair or wardrobe does not allow them to pass as uninteresting folks—are immensely prone to airport searches. Tucking herb in socks, under shoe soles, or in the waistband of boxer shorts is risky because the search is bound to happen. There is no failsafe method, but a solid bet for Trustafarians and other reasonable people who just want to relax is tightly wrapping that weed and nestling it in sweaty nether zones. No guard wants to put their hands there, especially if the recipient of handling looks like zombie-bitten Amy Winehouse. Other favorite Trustafarian options include standing behind a Muslim-seeming male at airport security (annoying him the whole time so he looks pissed and ready to hit someone) and leaving the weed at home because they are too scared to get caught and have Dad be really annoyed.

Picking a cruise can be tricky, but there is one that caters to Trustafarians. Jam Cruise is an annual high-seas adventure, featuring regular cruise destinations but with multi-venue jam band performances included. Setting sail every January, this cruise takes all the fun of an outdoor music festival and adds exclusivity, Caribbean islands, Trustafarian networking opportunities, and shuffleboard.

Jamaica

Jamaica is Impostafarian Mecca. A journey to Bob Marley's homeland is a right of passage, and with all the resorts, any sort of poverty and squalor can be overlooked. To try and trump other Trustafarians' visits, an Impostafarian may try to marry a local or take a bong hit with a Wailer, just for the story to tell.

Africa

Africa is a great place to visit too, though often instead of a trip to Ethiopia, Haile Selassie's homeland, Trustafarians will tend to opt for a Kenyan safari. To their credit, those Thomson's gazelles are just pure grace.

Australia

Once simply a spiritual rite of passage for Indigenous Australians, the walkabout is now an excuse for anyone to get lost in the Outback for a few months. With various chemical aids and probable dehydration, Trustafarians can easily access the Dreaming, a parallel reality full of sacred truths that informs the lives of the indigenous people. Trustafarians love sharing their more disturbing dreams, and they also love that the totemic religion reminds them of the blue aliens from *Avatar*.

The Far North

For many Trustafarians, interest in political matters peaked upon learning that Sarah Palin took part in aerial gunning. The idea of shooting something from a helicopter had never even occurred to most Trustafarians, and many frantically searched for a place to sign up for this excursion in Alaska. It is a real-life first-person-shooter game for those who can brave the cold. Fauxlanthropists are unlikely to take joy in the aerial slaughter, but they may very well have fun buzzing other choppers with their own protest helicopter.

SWEET RIDES

With the exception of some New Yorkers and some who borrow from Mom and Dad, Trustafarians accessorize their affected squalor by having a flashy set of wheels, which often gets hidden in a garage somewhere.

A very important accessory of many Trustafarian vehicles is the driver, who should have an attractive back of the head, and for straight, male Trustafarians, preferably looks a bit like Agent 99 from the *Get Smart* pilot. Many times though, the driver will end up being a meek old man who is a friend of the family and a terrible driver, but who Mom and Dad could not bear to fire, so now he drives their kid's car. Mom and Dad do not feel good about this, but they do feel safe and figure Junior is smart enough to fire the guy himself—or that is their hope.

Drivers are luxuries afforded to Trustafarians left over from a time when Mom wanted to sleep and the kids needed to get to school. As Trustafarians grow, they can make the mistake of getting too impatient while waiting the fifteen minutes between when they decide they want to go somewhere and when the driver arrives to pick them up. Also, in that time, they usually forget where they wanted to go and just end up going to Pinkberry, where the staff knows them by name.

> **NOTE:** Pinkberry is an upscale TCBY for those of you outside the New York and Los Angeles metropolitan areas.

Constant complaining about the driver's lag time will often lead to the driver's termination and a mandate that a Trustafarian drives his/her own car.

In What Cars Will You Find Trustafarians?

Fauxlanthropists have to have hybrids, or something entirely electric. They are taking a firm stand for Mother Gaia. The hybrid Honda Insight is a particular favorite, with its name that implies some sort of secret eco-intellect. The Prius is a classic stand-by. Brohemians and Impostafarians prefer their cars a bit tricked out but not so much that it might get them beaten up in every part of town. Impostafarians may opt for large dub wheels, which they ride on while listening to dub music. Brohemians enjoy a nice racing stripe, or gull-wing doors that remind them of a DeLorean. Diddlysquatters probably did not get their licenses and drive whatever they can borrow.

The word *dub* has a double meaning in the world of Trustafarians. First it refers to a type of music stemming from and remixing reggae. Second, it refers to a flashy car wheel with a diameter of twenty or more inches. If you are friends with a Trustafarian, you are bound to be smacked with one or the other.

TRUSTAFARIAN SPOTLIGHT ON

Lizzie Grubman

Now off the radar for the most part, publicist Lizzie Grubman has achieved the type of success any Trustafarian would be proud of. Daughter of a very successful lawyer, she attended New York City prep schools in her youth, taking a path that could have easily led her to Trustafarianism. She opted for more of a socialite route, but that does not detract from why the Trustafarians that do know of her, love her.

In 2001, she drove her SUV into a crowd of nightclub attendees in the Hamptons. As the story goes, the partiers had been pissing her off—so she took matters into her own rear tires. This is a fantasy crime of all Trustafarians who just got new SUVs. And Lizzie Grubman did it.

While she is decidedly not a Trustafarian, she holds true to their ideals, having served only a few weeks in prison, though she faced up to eight years. She also got out of a possible DUI conviction. If more Trustafarians knew of her (read the news), she would likely be prayed to.

Most Trustafarian cars will be black, though occasionally rust will make an ornate appearance. Mercedes, H2s, Bentleys, Aston Martins, Ferraris, Escalades, and Range Rovers are all fairly common, but then so are dilapidated '67 Beetles and skateboards. It really depends on a Trustafarian's need to compensate. Also if you spot something speeding down the highway that looks like it might morph into a Transformer, odds are good that a Trustafarian is driving.

FIGURE 2.d. *A completely earth-friendly vehicle, and favorite of Trustafarians, who can be seen carrying these almost anywhere*

TRUST FUN! | ## Spin the Globe, AKA Get Your Trustafarian to Buy a Globe and Then Spin It

Don't vicariously enjoy young retirement through your Trustafarian. Make him take you along as he travels to the exciting places that he does not fully appreciate.

STEP 1: Suggest a vacation, and then commit to a low spending cap, e.g., "Let's go on a three-week vacation. I have $100." You may use whatever amount you are comfortable with.

STEP 2: Spin the globe (or order a globe and return to the game in two to three business days). You may already have a destination in mind, but where is the fun in that? If you spin the globe, your Trustafarian's finger could end up anywhere. Anywhere! Though

FIGURE 2.e. *Spin carefully.*

CONTINUED ON NEXT PAGE

---

most likely it will get caught between the globe and the semi-meridian stand.

STEP 3: Ask your Trustafarian if he thinks you will be able to get there on your established budget. Odds are good that you will be considered a guest and have all expenses covered! If you are not, do not go.

STEP 4: Quit your job and prepare to live life as an intercontinental nomad for a few years.

NOTES: 1) You are going wherever that finger lands, so prepare for a trip to a landless portion of the Northern Pacific. 2) Your Trustafarian may hide weed on you to try to get it through airport security. Always watch his hands. 3) If your Trustafarian is caught with weed, it will be blamed on you, but if you make it through the airport, it should be a lovely trip.

Nap Culture
What the Trustafarian Does All Day

Imagine for a moment that you are a Trustafarian. Close your eyes. Go ahead. Close them, reader.

Imagine your dark but spacious bedroom around you. You just noticed you are awake, and you hear a strange sound like a bee buzzing. You realize it is your iPhone. Your arm slides out of the 1,000-thread-count Egyptian cotton sheet to find it. You open your eyes just a little bit (not your actual eyes, reader. Keep them closed). Into them, the dim afternoon light creeps. You can just make out the display on your phone, and it reads, "Incoming Call . . . Evil Bitch." You throw the phone down and wonder why the hell your mother is calling at 4:00 in the afternoon. The phone probably breaks, and you will have to get a new one at some point. That does not matter. The sheets are so soft. You stretch your shoulders and legs as you lie on your futon mattress in the middle of your unfurnished room. Your knee

touches something damp, but it probably is not anything to worry about. Either way, now you are awake.

Open your real eyes.

You have arrived at the make-or-break moment. It is the decision every Trustafarian makes:

Will I get up today?

A lot of times, there is indeed an affirmative response, but in that very first moment a Trustafarian realizes his/her complete freedom. It is 4:00 P.M. and anything is possible. If there is a to-do list, it is short, and the things that were scheduled before four o'clock can already be crossed off.

WHAT WILL A TRUSTAFARIAN GET UP FOR TODAY?

- Presents
- Food
- Sexcapades
- Desire to find a bed
- Weed

Where Is Your Trustafarian?

AT "WORK"

Paychecks come regularly from Mom and Dad—and probably on request as well—in amounts that easily cover rent and food. Insurance and student loans are all paid for by the company (which is Dad or Mom), so there is no real reason for a Trustafarian to take on a real job. Because of this, Trustafarians can be out of work in absolutely any field imaginable. They can be out-of-work movie stars, they can be out-of-work dentists, or they can be out-of-work astronauts. Every field is available for them not to be working.

Another way to cope with unemployment is to have a cover job or activity that a Trustafarian can use to make his/her parents think that their child is being productive.

TRUSTAFARIAN SKILLS IN ACTION

One Fauxlanthropist, who will remain nameless so as to avoid litigation, was recently walking from her gym to a Quiznos with a friend when her mother called. She told her mother that she could not talk because she was busy volunteering at the family-planning clinic. Then, after eating, she bought some jeans with some cool butt-pocket detail.

Every Trustafarian knows that these stipends come with some nominal stipulations. This "volunteer" knows that to keep the checks coming in, she must be seemingly active with some charity work. For months she has maintained her façade, but who can say how long it will last? "Many years" or "forever" would be appropriate guesses.

In searching for a job, Trustafarians need find something flexible enough to fit their whims and easy enough so as not to defeat the whole point of them being Trustafarians. Here are some tried-and-true Trustafarian employment opportunities:

TUTOR

A modicum of knowledge on any subject will do. The weekly commitment is only a few hours. Trustafarians are usually a lot smarter than they let on (or in the case of a degree-touting Brohemian, just as smart). College curriculum requirements finally come in handy as there are loads of slacking middle-schoolers out there who are failing fourth-grade science and third-grade reading. For these kids, Trustafarians are both teachers and role models, with valuable lessons to teach:

- How to make parents think that you are trying
- How to find answers to questions in the back of the book
- How a BA opens doors to a small world of employment options

Also, a tutor is really like a babysitter for when parents are too lazy to make their kids do homework. All a Trustafarian really has to do is sit there and make sure the kid looks like he/she is reading. By the time parents realize that their child's grades are not improving, the Trustafarian will have long since stopped showing up to work.

TOUR GUIDE

If they can find their way home, they can show people around. No matter where you live, there are bored people and tourists. Trustafarians can easily set up web pages that tout their tour-giving abilities and have their friends that they met once in foreign places sign the guest book, saying what wonderful tours they had. A tourist may only sign up every six months or so, but at least it is relatively honest work.

A special "herbal" or "green" tour may also be offered for those who are new to the area and need to know some of the unadvertised charm. Of course, this costs a lot more than the regular tour but comes highly recommended. Also, it supports local business.

Any Trustafarian with a boat, ship, yacht, or submarine can also give water tours or host fishing trips. These pull in even more money, but the IRS is more likely to catch on. Also, if a Trustafarian owns a boat, he/she may as well be a full-time skipper. It sounds like a job and they really do not have to do anything.

LANDLORD

This is the ultimate middleman for Mom and Dad's property buying. A Trustafarian can sit back, collect rent monthly, call in repair workers when needed, and occasionally, kick people out on a whim. They can choose tenants based on whom they think will make a better friend and then force their new friends to hang out with them, lest the new friends lose their housing. It is just like playing *The Sims* but with real people!

CAT SITTER

Friends go out of town all the time. For some reason, they may have taken comfort in pet ownership. With enough friends, Trustafarians do not even need a place of their own. (Of course, they will have one, just not use it.) In exchange for filling bowls with water and food once a day, Trustafarians are given shelter and the contents of the fridge that are about to expire.

If the cat dies early enough in the owner's vacation period, it becomes a vacation for the Trustafarian as well. Cats do not usually die though. Instead, they usually get lost or misplaced. Wacky high jinks will certainly ensue when a particularly loving pet owner returns to greet his/her new kitten.

FIGURE 3.b. *Be forewarned. Your Trustafarian friend does not want to see you upset when you get back from your trip, so Mr. Whiskers may look different, but he certainly will not look dead.*

FIGURE 3.c. *Claudia could not go with the family to the Vineyard because she had to stay home and take care of Stephanie, Lars, and Generalissimo Francisco Franco (pictured left to right).*

Even if it is only to a pet or a particularly needy houseplant, dedication to taking care of another is a painstaking, full-time task for a Trustafarian. It is also a great reason not to be able to go on family trips.

NOVELTY EX-PAT

This simple career move involves relocating somewhere foreign and being the crazy white kid. It is a very easy transition for the Impostafarians who are already extra unusual. (Where did that Jamaican accent come from, *mon?*)

Being a tour guide is an option in another country too, though couch surfing and schmoozing with locals are the preferred ways to work the exotic locale.

Being a novelty ex-pat can also be a career on its own. It also has the prestige of being an ambassadorial position. The Trustafarians aim to be cultural representatives for their own culture—or the culture of whoever they are pretending to be.

ETSY.COM SALESPERSON

This is one job path where a Trustafarian can take advantage of the virtually unregulated Internet marketplace. By simply attaching a few paperclips to some bottle caps or repurposing key chains to make earrings, the more artistically inclined Trustafarians can become Internet craftspeople. Websites like Etsy allow anyone to be an artist for potential pay. For many Trustafarians' parents, this will suffice as being an actual job. If a Trustafarian did not find a creative gene among the DNA he/she got from money-minded CEO parents, an alternative can be selling possessions on eBay.

FIGURE 3.d. *If you look at this picture and see a potential wallet, prom tux, or beer koozie, you just might have what it takes to sell your shoddy workmanship on the Internet!*

Generally, Trustafarians have a lot of stuff. If they can make their way to the UPS store or arrange for a Craigslist meetup, they can turn their junk into money! More money begets more junk. Employment continues!

A VOLUNTEER FOR SOMETHING

This one is pretty self-explanatory. Working for businesses that cannot afford to pay and do not have very many expectations is often an ideal situation for Trustafarians. Places like orphanages (homes for unwanted young people) and nursing homes (homes for unwanted old people) usually need volunteers to look cool in front of their tenants and act like they care. Trustafarians usually have the skills and the two to three hours of attention span needed to function well in this setting.

Volunteerism is something to which many people would love to subscribe, but they often sadly do not have the time. Being such societal successes, Trustafarians do. While some may use their volunteering only as a means to appease, many—such as the Fauxlanthropist—see it as a mission. Whether they prove themselves useful or just further hassles in the life of a not-for-profit, they are helping people.

TEMP WORKER

Nothing says "accommodation" more than having a boss who understands you are going to quit whenever you feel like it.

A very good place for a Trustafarian to work temporarily is Mom's or Dad's office. This combines two of Trustafarian life's biggest hassles: working, even though it is unnecessary, and socializing with parents. It may multiply displeasure, but it certainly consolidates time spent on these activities.

A new hassle may arise for Trustafarians in the temporary world. Many do not have the appropriate wardrobe for an office setting. Still, an afternoon of shopping with Mom's credit card can provide the right duds for that shabby-chic look.

ACTOR/MODEL/DESIGNER/MUSICIAN/PAINTER

On first glance, it may appear that talent is essential to being an artist, but the real key ingredients are time and money. You might be a talented sculptor, but if you do not have the means to acquire a three-by-four-foot chunk of marble and the time to hack it into something, you are stuck working in human resources.

The Hilton sisters are great examples. Here are two young women who aspire to leave their marks on culture. There may be more talented fashion designers and actresses—there are certainly less talented fashion designers and actresses—but because they have the means, they get the chance to make expensive cut-off jeans and campy, horror, rock musicals.

YOGA INSTRUCTOR/DANCE TEACHER

A few classes and a sketchy certification program are all that are needed for this job sector. Malnourishment and limberness are fairly common Trustafarian traits that serve well here. Dance does not have to be anything formal, just movement. People will pay a lot of money to be told to move around in a room full of mirrors. Similarly, people will pay a lot of money to stretch in a very hot room. These are healthy and fun activities, and Trustafarians, who are too impatient to learn, will often find ways to teach others what they think they know.

PRIEST/PRIESTESS

There is not any way a Trustafarian will become a church leader in any major religion, but there are plenty of niche religions that meet in garages, park amphitheaters, and the attics of actual churches for which anyone may become a priest. If you could ask the ancient Aztecs, they would tell you that a strange, charismatic, and well-funded white guy arriving out of nowhere is likely to gut you to your religious core.

Trustafarians will enjoy their priesthood because it will subconsciously remind them of the blind following their parents have in the realms of work and society. They also get to make up things like commandments and secret rituals. There is nothing unentertaining about interpreting God for a room full of people who have to listen to you. Science becomes a barrel from which to pick and choose. Anything can be worshiped. Mountains, colors, refrigerators are all potential deities, and no matter what is chosen, it is protected by the First Amendment of the U.S. Constitution.

Thomas "Baller" Cuttingham is a Trustafarian and Priest of what he calls "Visceral Discordianism." He provided *The Trustafarian Handbook* with this list of commandments to illustrate how Trustafarian ideals can work in tandem with structured religion.

I. God is love. Love is money.

II. All words are meant to be spoken. That is why they are words.

III. Remember to sleep through Sunday.

IV. Sort of honor thy real mother and father when they are around thee.

V. Don't get caught for stuff.

VI. Pick an ironic Confirmation name.

VII. We will be having Confirmations.

VIII. Is that 10 yet?

IX. 9 is the new whatever.

ENTREPRENEUR

All they need is seed money and an idea. Having copious free time allows the mind to wander in some incredible directions. Certain herbs help too. In an inspirational flash of what seems like a good idea at the time, money can become more money and Dad will be forced to take back all the disapproving things he has ever said. An office is quickly bought and a web designer is hired to design something—though no one is quite sure what.

Ben Goldhirsh

Ben is the son of Bernie Goldhirsh, founder of the monthly magazine *Inc*. Ben started *GOOD Magazine* . . . with his college friends . . . using a trust fund. The magazine tag is, "for people who give a damn." No one knows how much a damn is, and no one really knows what this magazine is about. Still, people read it. One very good thing about *GOOD*, is that all subscription money goes to charity. This makes for good media coverage, and it makes Goldhirsh a Fauxlanthropist's most eligible bachelor.

Is he a Trustafarian himself? Well, the magazine was started with unearned seed money and it only comes out quarterly. Apparently *monthly* just takes too much effort.

TRUST FUN! | ## The Business Plan!

Here is a fun idea for you and your Trustafarian: start a business! This is especially useful if you are equally as out of work as the Trustafarian but do not have monthly stipends that make it worthwhile.

STEP 1: Get in a confined space with your Trustafarian, who is stoned out of his/her mind.

STEP 2: Suggest a game, one in which you come up with euphemisms for genitalia.

STEP 3: Play the game. This can last for hours! Amazing! You will probably want to stop before you both pass out though, just in case. When you are about through, pause the game right after the Trustafarian says something relatively inoffensive. Take "Briny Sea" as an example.

STEP 4: Say, "You know what? Briny Sea would be an awesome name for a store!" Your Trustafarian will of course agree because you are

CONTINUED ON NEXT PAGE

enthusiastic, and that is fun! He/she may ask, "What would we sell?" In this rare case, you treat it like a Mad Lib and say the first noun that comes to mind.

STEP 5: Say this line exactly: "That would be fucking awesome, only . . . I don't have the money for that." You can add a sigh if you are feeling theatrical. At this point your Trustafarian will either show you a credit card or something he/she thinks is a credit card. The Trustafarian may also pick up a phone to call Mom. Either way, proceed to Step 6.

STEP 6: Open your business. Give yourself a high pay rate. You may be able to get a few days' salary before the Trustafarian gets tired of work. You then can carry on by yourself or start this process again.

TRUSTAFARIAN SPOTLIGHT ON

Ivanka Trump

Though not a Trustafarian herself, Trump exemplifies certain Trustafarian ideals. She is the daughter of the Donald, and she has managed to snag the title of vice president in her mid-twenties. That seems like a lot of work for Trustafarians, until they realize she works for her Dad's company. She models too because she can afford to be that beautiful.

Not too many socialite-heiresses will be highlighted in this handbook, but some must be represented, as money affords an easy road upon which Trustafarians can also ride, and these ladies are in the public eye. Many Trustafarians go unnoticed.

Trump's success, winning a sweet career, under the auspices of her father, teaches all Trustafarians that family is important, and must not be too eagerly forsaken.

Where Is Your Trustafarian?

NAPTIME

Trustafarians usually keep hours that resemble a 4:00 P.M. to 5:00 A.M. day with a solid eleven-hour sleep period. Sometimes things like yoga class will get in the way of the late rise time, but there is help for the early riser and indeed all Trustafarians. It is a sweet little collection of respites called *Naptime*.

After a couple of hours of working or pretending to work, a Trustafarian will desire to rest the body and forget what just happened. It is important to take the time to nap because there are just too many hours in the day to be actively occupied.

EXCELLENT NAPPING PLACES

- **The Entryway:** If the first thing they are going to do when they get home is nap, they may as well do it in the first place they step.
- **The Bed:** It does not have to be theirs, and it does not have to be real.
- **The Cab:** Nothing makes a taxi driver happier than idling for a while with a snoozer in the back and the meter running.
- **The Family Dinner Table:** No one was talking anyway.
- **The Shower:** That hot water from the massage setting on the showerhead is just too wonderful.
- **Landings:** Some staircases are just not meant to be conquered in a single shot.

Communal napping is very common too. When a group of friends or acquaintances runs out of things to talk about, they fall asleep. Normally something like television could stave off the unconsciousness, and while there is a fifty-two-inch flat screen, it is not hooked up because the Trustafarian owner views TV as a pure marketing tool and claims there is not anything good to watch. Group enjoyment of alcohol and marijuana can also aid in collective napping prowess.

Naptime is a great way to relieve stress that comes from parents. It also helps stave off any worry about the future, allowing Trustafarians to truly live or sleep in the moment.

Naptime also encompasses passing out. This can, of course, take place anywhere at any time.

Where Is Your Trustafarian?

JAIL

This is the one time parents find out where their Trustafarians are without having to call first. A Trustafarian may contact them directly or use his speed-dial-accessed lawyer as a go-between. Any number of trivial things can land Trustafarians in jail. Police, like most people, are simply jealous of their existence and try to crush their spirits whenever possible. Crimes may include refusing to pay for a $7 milkshake because the cashier wouldn't break a $100 bill, trying to buy weed from a cop who was not undercover, or refusing to move from one of Stonehenge's megaliths, where a very important nap was in progress.

Parents very likely have the bail money orders already drawn up and made out to the local detention centers. The smart Trustafarian will carry these around in his/her wallet.

FIGURE 3.e. *A free pass, one of six carried around at all times. Bail may be more expensive but there may be a limit set on the amount of a money order. Check with your local department of corrections. Police officers and mall cops are now invited to "bring it."*

Where Is Your Trustafarian?

THE BAR

If you enter a bar and think, "With all the poorly dressed young people in here, the drinks must be cheap!" only to be confronted with a $14 starting price for martinis, you have found yourself inside a Trustafarian bar. If you want further proof, look around for things like board games and some sort of obscure European table sport. Also check to see if there is an inebriated Impostafarian at the bar trying to explain to the bartender how to make a layered shooter in Rasta colors.

TRUST FUN! | ## Drink your Gnarly Marley

Fun people love alcohol. When you start to shy away from the really hard stuff and lose your taste for beer, you get into the fun liqueurs that can be accessorized! A Gnarly Marley is easy to make, and it can be considered a tribute. Show your Impostafarian that you care by making one of these okay-tasting shooters.

STEP 1: Delicately layer a red band of grenadine in the bottom of the glass.
STEP 2: On top of that, carefully add some strongly spiked eggnog, or some sort of premade egg cream liqueur.
STEP 3: Add a green band of crème de menthe.

You have now poured yourself a Rasta-inspired shooter in the bold colors of the Ethiopian nation, recognizable to Rastafarians everywhere!

FIGURE 3.f. *Your shot glass is full of flavor and meaning.* **Grenadine:** *It is red, too often spilled and a mess to clean up, just like the blood of man.* **Eggnog:** *It is a little bit yellow and only available around Christmas when you should be peaceful, happy, and aware of what you should really value.* **Crème de menthe:** *It is refreshing, just like waking up in a pile of dewy grass, so this represents the Earth.*

Some people also like to top this shooter with a tropical splash of rum, light it on fire, and try to down it via straw before the straw melts. To some observers, who try their very best to remain objective, this seems like burning the Ethiopian flag—not cool.

Bars are frequent hangouts for Trustafarians because it gets them out of the apartment and there is usually Red Stripe. It also gives them a chance to meet and mingle with like-minded, if not like-funded, individuals.

Where Is Your Trustafarian?

SHOPPING

Looking like a Trustafarian is hard work! Each outfit has to say, "I'm rich enough that wearing this is ironic, but not so rich that it's offensive—really." The breakdown of what they are buying will be covered later, but here it is important to understand how much of an effort shopping is. Cities generally do not take the time to zone a thrift district. Often these stores will be miles and even hours apart. Sure, every so often, like on Twenty-third Street in New York City, you will get a string of two or three in a row, but then you also have to go down to the Village and then to Brooklyn to make sure you are seeing all the new old duds. It can take hours or even a whole Trustafarian day.

Thrift shopping is frenzied and even sometimes violent. Quality vintage threads go fast. Worst of all, they are often put in the store windows a week before they are available to buy. If everyone knows in advance about a hot item, there will be a rush to get it as soon as the store opens the day it goes on sale.

The thrift stores of Trustafarian neighborhoods do not cater to the particularly thrifty. Prices will be on par with clothes that never belonged to dead people at all.

Impostafarians and Fauxlanthropists are the biggest thrift store shoppers. They will also venture into the boutique stores that cater to Bohemian styles. You will find the other Trustafarians in your typical mall stores, though never in an Abercrombie & Fitch. (You may think a Brohemian would fit in at the preppy retail chain, but he/she will not have the body to pull off the clothes in a way that looks appropriate by anyone's standards.) Diddlysquatters wear that same ratty sweater that they got in seventh grade and, perhaps, pants.

Where Is Your Trustafarian?

OFF THE GRID

Trustafarians have an uncanny ability to lose track of themselves for periods of time. No one is quite sure where they go or what happens while they are there. It is just part of their charm.

Some of the world's greatest art has gone missing for decades at a time, and when it surfaces again, it is loved even more.

Where Is Your Trustafarian?

DOING CHARITY WORK

For those who choose to practice it—namely the Fauxlanthropists—charity work can be the most rewarding or parentally mandated part of the day.

Young kids get sick a lot and it is often really sad. Fauxlanthropists are not immune to that pathos. From visiting those tormented tots in the hospital wing named after their grandfathers to throwing some sort of wonderful wheelchair prom, there are plenty of fun and relatively hands-off ways to help.

Who does not love cutting ribbons?

Fauxlanthropists are also the Trustafarians most likely to have an artistic streak, since to be an artist, one should have some sort of purpose. Charity can often count as that purpose. The art itself does not have to have meaning if it can be sold and the proceeds can be given to charity. Thus, from aimless artist chrysalides, Fauxlanthropists are born.

To get an audience, Fauxlanthropists, with limited numbers of actual friends, will often have to extend event invitations to their parents' rich peers, who will only attend a gallery opening or a play reading if it benefits the less fortunate. Getting people to travel to the artistic part of town to see portraits done in menstrual blood or painted with the ashes of dead people is a difficult sell on its own, but charity justifies the artistic experience. Because of this relationship, much of "charity work" time can be spent developing artistic craft. Three hours of screaming into a camera while being wrapped in an American flag may therefore be considered charitable. It may seem strange, but remember, if the showing of the video brings in money to fight leukemia, it is charity.

> The final amount collected from Fauxlanthropists' charitable donations is always less than expected, generally due to the cost of celebrity endorsements and those giant novelty checks.

Where Is Your Trustafarian?

SMOKING UP

You saw this coming. Marijuana may be enjoyed solo or in a group. Nothing says brotherhood (or sisterhood) in the Trustafarian world as much as guys or gals sharing their weed.

Where Is Your Trustafarian?

ON THEIR COUCH . . . CONVINCING PEOPLE TO BRING THEM THINGS

This is done for many reasons. It could be as simple as not wanting to put on pants or as complex as a masked plea for companionship. It can also be done out of frustration or just the need to detoxify from stress. Their minds can relax while a friend or relative reminds them of their younger days by serving them immediately, when requested. Whatever the motivation, text messages will be sent and phone calls will be made, asking for things outside of the Trustafarian's immediate reach.

A request might go out for milk because a Trustafarian decided to make waffles and is pissed off at a bowl of Bisquick and lack of foresight. Alcohol is a common request, and so is weed, because a Trustafarian does not want to deal with the hassles of arranging a pickup—which would have actually been a shorter text message.

POPULAR TRUSTAFARIAN TEXT REQUESTS

- "Pimple midback. Not reachable. Can u help?"
- "U want to text me about something???"
- "Just saw japanese gameshow bring eggs hamburg n mannequin now"

People will deliver because Trustafarians always have charisma in stock, though they often hide it or choose not to use it, opting for a more brooding style of discourse. They learned charisma from their parents, who have successfully used it to make their fortunes. Also from their parents, Trustafarians learned to go after what they want and to not stop until they get it or find someone else to get it for them.

A Short Day's Journey Into Night

Being a Trustafarian really requires a commitment to oneself. With so few active hours in the day, time can be spent only on things that are truly important to the individual Trustafarians. With limited multitasking capabilities, many find that some tasks, like maintaining interpersonal relationships and staying conscious through conversations, simply do not fit on the daily agenda.

Some people accuse the Trustafarians of propagating negative stereotypes about trust fund kids—that they are too selfish or too lazy. Trustafarians are not concerned about how they are perceived. They do not care what you or anyone else thinks because they know who they are. Their day is intentionally jam-packed with Trustafarian-friendly activities because if they had too much free or awake time, they might start to second-guess themselves.

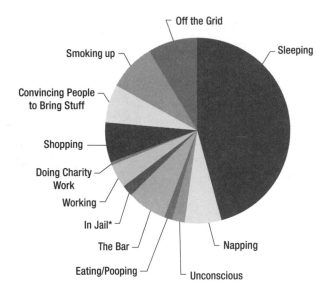

FIGURE 3.g. **BREAKDOWN OF THE TRUSTAFARIAN DAY**
On days when Trustafarians do not get arrested, the jail time portion of the pie graph may be added to "sleeping."

Ganja

Because Jah Says So

For decades there has been fervid debate over the use of marijuana, which has been in use for many thousands of years, the majority of which were debate free. Thanks to the heat of that nascent conflict, a thick, tangy smoke has finally begun to envelop protesters, and with increasing frequency, cannabis is slowly becoming either decriminalized or allowed for medical use. It has come a long way from being viewed as simply a gateway drug to jazz music, but there is still enough cultural contention that Mom and Dad will not be pleased with a child's recreational usage. It is a Trustafarian's way to relax and rebel.

FIGURE 4.a. *A true Trustafarian friend*

ganja (gän´jə) n.

Rastafarian: cannabis intended for smoking to heighten spirituality and cleanse the mind

Trustafarian: a sought-after way to say "pot" without looking like one is trying too hard

Parents of Trustafarians: (term not spoken) black people's Klonopin

Somewhere around age twelve, budding Trustafarians will be given their first opportunities to buy some weed from an enterprising upperclassman. This purchase will be met with great eagerness and cost all of the cash currently on hand. For some, the eagerness is quite real. Marijuana is a long awaited step toward being a grownup and telling society that they can take some part of its anatomy and shove it up another. For many though, the enthusiasm is a façade. They wonder if the drug will hurt them, or they fear not being in control of their bodies. Some never grow out of it. Some of the most burnt-out, mellow-acting, Dylan-spinning, thirty-eight-year-old Trustafarians have never inhaled. They live in a comfort zone, and always fear change of any kind.

For certain Trustafarians the spiritual call of cannabis is impossible to ignore. Of course, some are too scared to try it and would rather just mimic the lifestyle. The Rastafarian belief that God is okay with the herb leads many to believe that this is the God for them. For many religions and houses of worship, there is a lesson to be learned here.

Tokers and Jokers

The amount of experience a Trustafarian has with marijuana can generally be determined by his/her Trustafarian type. A toker is the most experienced and savvy weed user, and the Trustafarians most likely to get that label are the Fauxlanthropists. Many people assume Impostafarians would be, but this is one instance in which the "imposter" portion of their nomenclature comes into play. They are isolated. Often, true Rastas do not accept them, and the Impostafarians would prefer to be alone rather than with people who do not exhibit the traits they associate with true Rastafarians. The amount of weed they can access is limited, and when they get it, they are not sure what to do with it, beyond what the Internet tells them.

Fauxlanthropists, in contrast, have a diverse array of acquaintances—acquired through their attempts at charitable work—that may include artists and drug lords. It is really an impressive spectrum. When visiting a toker Fauxlanthropist at home, you will experience the air of expertise upon entering. A Fauxlanthropist will generally flop on the couch and light up. Within minutes you will be passed a svelte swathe of evenly rolled weed along with a monogrammed Zippo lighter. Conversation will proceed involving anything but what you are smoking.

Jokers are most likely either Impostafarians or Brohemians whose bros are just as unknowledgeable about weed as they are. When one of these Trustafarians greets you at the door, the hand that is not on the doorknob will probably be holding a large bag of weed, and he/she will be wearing a big dopey smile with eyebrows raised as if to say, "Par-taayyy!"

An Impostafarian may alternatively invite you over to listen to some Bob Marley, watch *Cool Runnings*, and eat some brownies, but there will be no sign whatsoever of any weed. At that point, it is up to you to bring the party or find another one.

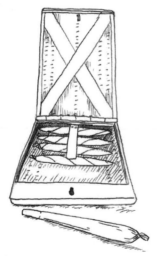

FIGURE 4.b. *A joint rolled by a Fauxlanthropist*

FIGURE 4.c. *A joint rolled by an Impostafarian*

ganjaphile (gän´jə-fīl´) n.
English: a person who actively makes marijuana (ganja) use and appreciation part of daily life
Trustafarian: Me!

TRUST FUN! | ## Being Dealt a Joker

If you have worked hard to snag yourself a Trustafarian only to find that you have a joker on your hands, do not fret: there is plenty of fun to be had!

STEP 1: Be sure. On occasion a toker will have a bad day and be really eager about his/her herb. You do not want to proceed with the following steps if your buddy is in fact a toker. Try saying something like "this is fucking good dope." A toker will know right away that he is being tested and will probably slap you—very much worth it because from then on it will be smooth sailing. A joker will respond with "Yeahhh" or "Is 'dope' a thing again?" Either way, you have them now.

STEP 2: Establish dominance. With a few exciting stories—real or made up—about your past with Mary Jane, you will gain your joker's respect. He/she will see this as an opportunity to transition from joker to toker.

STEP 3: Let it all go to your head. Catch him/her in the act, but do not let on that you are savvy. Ask unanswerable questions like "Why is this weed so good? Is it mac and cheese or is it dolphin gravy?" You *will* get answers!

STEP 4: Re-educate. Leave your mark on culture. The joker is looking to you for leadership and will certainly pass what he/she learns to other joker friends. Enjoy this.

CONTINUED ON NEXT PAGE

Introduce more new phrases to the lexicon. "Tooting the grouch" and "Marrying your fuzzy cousin" are just waiting to be born.

Do not stop at just words though. Introduce actions. Listen to how the weed sounds. Bring it very close to your ear so you can really hear it. Watch your Trustafarian do the same, and try your best not to laugh. It really makes for a fun night, so never be too upset that your Trustafarian is not too experienced with his/her ganja.

If you happen to be sexually attracted to your Trustafarian, you can use this opportunity to do things like passing smoke mouth-to-mouth or just licking each other to get "a savory taste on your tongue to fully enhance the quality of the weed."

Five Words Actually Used for Marijuana *By Trustafarians That Use Marijuana*	*Five Words* Not *Actually Used For* Marijuana *By Trustafarians That Use Marijuana*
1. Weed	1. Marijuana
2. Herb	2. Dope
3. Bud	3. Mary Jane/MJ
4. Grass	4. Reefer
5. Ganja	5. Wacky Tobacky

The word *pot* was not mentioned on either list. It is a commonly used adjective (pothead, pot brownies), but has lost its footing when it comes to the nominative form. The number 420 is also common, but its wide spread use is fairly limited to Internet personals and roommate listings. Consequently, the date 4/20 is a very popular date for pot parties and pop rock album releases.

LESSER GANJAPHILES

Following the Fauxlanthropists in spliff savvy are the Diddlysquatters. For both groups there is a tremendous spectrum of ganja to be understood and enjoyed. Some exchange words like *headies* and *hydro*, and in listening to them, you really feel that you are in the presences of connoisseurs. It works to legitimatize the lifestyle. A raging alcoholic who runs a vineyard, swirls his drink, and uses phrases like "good vintage" is readily accepted and even lauded. A little knowledge goes a long way and helps to show that a person really has a respect for his/her craft.

Diddlysquatters beat out the Brohemians in terms of ganja savvy because they have ample alone time to devote to the discovery and practice of nuances in marijuana manner. You may be treated to an entirely unique experience when visiting them. Elaborate or creative bongs are also common, and even function as a rare status symbol within the Diddlysquatter community—which by definition is no community at all, but rather a disconnected assortment of loners who are vaguely aware of one another. With their copious amount of free time and lots of cannabis-inspired creativity, the stage is always set for an impressive show.

Many Diddlysquatters prefer using bongs as ways to cool, filter, and/or amass smoke. There are many types of this water pipe to choose from. One popular variety is the gravity bong. If you are not familiar, this device uses changes in pressure caused by the vertical movement of an inverted container seated in a bucket of water. The name

FIGURE 4.d. *With the right hardware, anything can be a bong.*

"gravity bong" is a bit strange. Much like Grape-Nuts, guinea pigs, and Providence, RI, it was named by someone who did not really know what he/she was talking about. Gravity only works to keep the water in the bucket, so by that naming convention you might take a dip in the gravity pool or relax to the sound of gravity ocean waves crashing.

The aesthetic downside to a gravity bong is that it looks like something a janitor whipped up using items from his closet. Water bongs, which also have water, are great alternatives for Diddlysquatters and other Trustafarians to add creative elbowroom. For these, any container will do as long as the former contents were not poisonous. It just needs to be airtight and water tight, with the exception of some key openings: the carb hole, the stem hole, and the mouthpiece.

Soda cans and bottles are common water bong choices, but their use connotes hastiness. Diddlysquatters are in no rush; they have nowhere to be. It is possible that more creativity and energy will go into their herbal experiences than any other events in life. It can even border on lavish. Container choices range from exotic fruit to intense and even frightening Rube Goldberg devices, all with promise of delivering an exciting and relatively unforgettable bong-hitting experience. These bongs, however, are quickly outmoded as Diddlysquatters, perhaps in a chemically altered state, dream up bigger and better designs. Should there be any stress caused by this pursuit of the ultimate hit, relief comes built in.

There are many options for those Trustafarians who choose not to be creative and wish to use their financial backing to establish ganja status. Zongs are a type of glass bong that zig and zag their way to increased volume in a small amount of space while adding an architectural element that is reminiscent of a fun day at the water park. Hookahs are also elaborate water pipes that function very similarly. They are always ornate and can often have several hoses stemming out of the pipe body so friends can join in the fun, if only the Diddlysquatters had some. Brohemians love them. Hookahs also have sexy hardware like gaskets that are noticeably lacking from other water pipes. The drawback is that they can be hard to hide if civic-minded parents or parole officers plan on making visits. Of course, the default justification to owning a hookah is that it is "only being used to smoke fruity tobacco," the appletini of the smoking world.

> **chillum** (chĭl´ŭm) n.
> *Rastafarian*: a cone-shaped pipe for smoking cannabis
> *Trustafarian*: (stereotypical) Ebonics word for "children" (often used to show cultural awareness)

As a Drug

You may be hostile toward Trustafarians for making your neighborhood unaffordable or for smelling like a dead person, but can you really hold recreational cannabis use against them?

They have a lot of stress that cannot be worked out through conventional means:

There is ample funding provided for an upper-class style of existence, which they resolutely believe they do not want. There are parents and financial managers constantly belaboring points about how people should act and spend their time on Earth. There are people who they idolize and aspire to be like but who will never accept them for who they are. There are disapproving people all around who expect the Trustafarians to feel bad about the opportunities they were given. There are cable guys who show up late. There is pre-empted television programming due to sporting and current events. There are massive war protests to which they were not invited. There are surprisingly few green M&M's in the package, and there is exceptional difficulty finding someone else to share the double occupancy rate on the Antarctic cruise.

All that tension builds in the mind, in the shoulders, and on the back of Trustafarians. A little weed is all they need. It can even be shared with friends. It becomes a bonding experience where words and activeness are unnecessary.

How many times have you been in this situation?

```
YOU: What do you want to do tonight?
FRIEND: I don't know. What do you want to do?
YOU: I don't know. . . . What do you want to do?
FRIEND: I want to "Shoop."
YOU: What is that?
FRIEND: Dated song reference.
YOU: Really? Is it?
FRIEND: Don't be sarcast—
YOU: Tell me what you want to do!
```

Planning an evening can be hard work. Trustafarians and other tokers have found a hard-to-beat alternative:

```
FRIEND: Here.
YOU: Thanks.
```

Those two words of dialogue could easily be replaced by indicative head tilts. This is, of course, not meant to be an invitation to go out and find a local ganja distributor. It is meant, like the rest of this book, to illustrate the qualities of Trustafarians that make them so successful. Here they have alleviated stress, fostered fraternity (when fraternity is sought after), and potentially found God in a single step.

Through cannabis, every banal object can become art. Metacognition is not only realized, but also understood. People who were believed to be intolerable finally become not so bad. If you have ever resented a Trustafarian for any of this, shame on you. You may not agree with the course, but that vacation destination is pretty awesome.

It should be noted that there is no concrete understanding of cannabis's long-term effect on the body, so there is no tangible reason to detest it.

Not all Trustafarians are ganjaphiles or even casual ganja users, but they all have some on standby just in case someone doubts their devil-may-care attitude.

As a Food Group

Tetrahydrocannabinol, or THC, is the pharmacologically active chemical in cannabis. The most common way to make it edible is by using the ever-tasty refrigerator staple, butter, to absorb it. This handbook will not explain how to make pot butter, as it can go wrong and there will already be enough litigation troubles from the Trustafarians. (Although, you probably already know that about five sticks of butter and some cheesecloth will get you on your way.)

FIGURE 4.e. *Indulgence the way only Trustafarians can. Maine Lobster drenched in drawn pot butter redefines any clambake.*

Pot butter is a butter substitute and can be used in anything in which butter is used, taking its exalted place, perched high atop the food pyramid. Most commonly it is slipped into recipes for bakery sweets such as warm and gooey chocolate chip cookies or brownies. It brings new life to corn, whether popped or on the cob. Less commonly it will

---

be used to make a nice scampi. Its versatility really helps bring new talent to the kitchen. Without it, Trustafarians would exist mainly on take-out and Ramen Noodles. The level of culinary skill they achieve will often pleasantly surprise parents and friends alike.

As Means of Ingratiation

Ganja on its own is a great equalizer, like eating hotdogs or being sent to Gitmo. No matter who people were before they showed up, they share the experience as peers.

The external want of a Trustafarian is, of course, to blend in. Impostafarians can get other people stoned to a point where Rastafarian legitimacy is no longer doubted. Fauxlanthropists can sprinkle it around like Tinker Bell and then try to make the world have happy thoughts. Brohemians can patch up any falling-out they may have had with the bros. Diddlysquatters can barter it in exchange for having a friend make dinner, wash dishes, or kill a roach, and Heirasites can ingratiate themselves to real Trustafarian ganjaphiles. For however brief a respite, Trustafarians are associated with the green in their plastic baggies, not the green in their calfskin leather wallets.

OUT-DOOBY THE COMPETITION

Trustafarians adoption of weed culture seems almost perfect, just like the Trustafarians, but there is often a snag. As much as they are driven to appear as part of the Everyman society (or for Impostafarians, the every-black-man society), certain subconscious instincts run deeper. Trustafarians will usually drop subtle hints of their real value. An easy and common way to achieve this is by assisting the rolling of a joint with paper currency.

Here, a smoke circle becomes like a poker table. Each person has to out-bid the other. Quickly, a room of eager smokers becomes a frenzied group, searching for the highest denominations in their wallets, assuming they have not lost them again. There are no winners in this contest, only losers.

Most Fauxlanthropists, whose smoking buddies are more likely to be non-Trustafarians, and Diddlysquatters, who effectively use the Internet, know that rolling a joint by using only their dexterity earns higher respect than using any sort of monetary aid. Still, some cannot help themselves.

TRUST FUN! | Roll a J with a Franklin

A lot of rich people wonder how this is done, so here are the details . . .

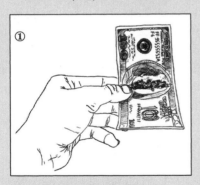 

STEP 1: Fill this non-president bill with your finest herb. Fold the bill in half and begin rolling.
STEP 2: Insert your rolling paper between the valuable bill and the weed.

CONTINUED ON NEXT PAGE

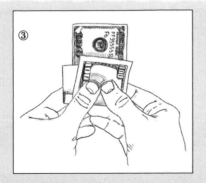

STEP 3: Use this incredible monetary sum to roll the paper around the weed. Continue until it is ready to lick and stick.

STEP 4: Remove the joint from the $100 bill, which is the highest-valued paper currency currently being circulated in the United States, being careful to angle it so that everyone can see just how much it is worth.

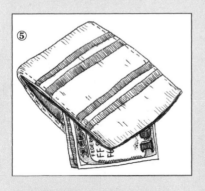

STEP 5: Accidentally drop the c-note, which could easily buy over ninety-two four-piece nuggets, inclusive of taxes, and hope that a buddy points out that your money (or the equivalent to the gross national product of some impoverished nations) is lying on the floor. If no one is observant enough to spot this, wait a few minutes and casually point out that someone must have dropped it. Then discover—feign discovery—that one of the many in your wallet is missing. Point this out as well. Pick it up and tuck it back in your wallet so that it's visible.

Job well done! Relax and enjoy that superior joint.

WHERE THEY ARE HIDING THEIR WEED

If you are a parent, you can confiscate it. If you are a friend, you can find it when they are passed out.

- Hollowed-out Bible
- Second bathroom, used as closet
- Second apartment, used as closet
- That other trash can near the bed
- Taped underneath their pizzelle maker
- Hair
- It is not hidden
- Growing with the other plants in the rooftop garden
- Among the imported loose-leaf teas
- Taped behind the Wii/Xbox 360
- Inside unworn dress socks
- The Akita ate it—no, really

High Fashion
The Stunning Return of Cannabis

The spectrum of Trustafarian garb and accessories is actually quite vast, and almost anything goes as long as it can be bought on an impulse or cause Mom and Dad to shake their heads in disbelief.

The Clothing

HEMP

There is a special type of cannabis that is not smoked. In fact, it is cultivated for fabric (and many other purposes), and it is called *hemp*. This plant is just so versatile! Naysayers with vested interests in the forestry industry may disagree, but from organic T-shirts to tote bags and bracelets, hemp is a great way to drape the body with flowing, natural fabric. Trustafarians often see leather and synthetic fabrics as vulgar and supportive of exploitative industries. They see hemp as perfection.

> Leather wallets do not count as actual leather in the minds of Trustafarians. Wallets hold money, a necessary evil, so it is okay if the container is evil too.

Trustafarians understand that for some reason or another, hemp is good for the environment. After all, if paper were made from hemp, fewer trees would be slaughtered. For the ganja-philes, it is a way to show dedication to the herb that they love. With the exception of the stiffly braided waist and wrist wear, hemp clothing is often indistinguishable from other natural fabrics.

Some Trustafarians will make an effort to find an article of clothing adorned with a pot leaf or Bob Marley's head to include in their daily ensembles. For Impostafarians, this style of dressing is to be considered spiritual, and akin to dressing up for church.

THE BAJA

It is unisex. It keeps them warm. It has a hood in case it rains or they would like to brood. Also going by the name *jerga*, this simple woven pullover is as fashionable as it is a shirt. Almost always there is a pocket in the front where hands can be warmed, snacks can be stored, and iPods can be futzed with. It is also accepted that when a male's hands are in his Baja pocket, he is caressing his definitively male parts through the layers of fabric. There may even be a hole in there.

FIGURE 5.a. *An ensemble composed of only one material: hemp. Sandals, bag, bracelet, tank top, hat, belt, and skirt were provided by Mother Earth, herself. Bra was not provided by anyone.*

FIGURE 5.b. *The Baja is an iconic piece of Trustafarian leisure/formal wear, perfect for Phish concerts and Dad's next wedding.*

RECYCLED CLOTHING

Recycling clothing goes far beyond chopping the sleeves off an old sweater and turning them into arm warmers—though they are timeless Trustafarian pieces. They do not harm the environment. (Fauxlanthropists feel good about that.) They can be acquired without having to leave the apartment. (Diddlysquatters feel great about that.) By mutilating that unworn sweater your aunt got you four Christmases ago, you can really get a sense of Trustafarian ingenuity. Please take about four minutes to make some arm warmers.

TRUST FUN! | **Arm Warmer Break**

Arm warmers are a great way to say, "I've got this bitchin' witticism T-shirt I wanna wear, but it's awfully cold out." They are a particular favorite of the Trustafarians, who generally took a trip at some point during high school to New York City and saw the musical *Rent*. Aside from taking away valuable lessons about life, love, and lesbians, budding Trustafarians also took away some fashion ideas to pepper their wardrobe with that no-longer-existent East Village angst. If you spot a Trustafarian with leopard print boots, blue vinyl pants, a bold stripy scarf or cat ears, you can bet it is something he/she took away from this former Broadway show. They will not admit this. They will sing *Seasons of Love* in the car though. Look for it at red lights.

If you have picked out a sweater that you enjoy for the sleeves but not much else, you are ready to make your arm warmers.

STEP 1: Delicately sheer off the sleeves from the main body of the sweater. It is important not to have a jagged-looking end to the arm warmer because people will think less of you.

CONTINUED ON NEXT PAGE

STEP 2: Turn those sleeves around. It is not as straightforward as you thought! The tapered, former wrist of the sweater is going to be the part of the arm warmer that sits near your bicep. The former shoulder will now have a gentle flared effect over your wrist.

STEP 3: Slip into them and enjoy!

Hopefully your arm warmer break was enjoyable. Moving on, another obvious way to recycle clothing is just to buy it second-hand. Any clothing that a Trustafarian buys from a thrift store has been paid for at least twice, so the value of the clothes immediately goes up. Each stitch has some history and mystery to it. All sorts of wonderful thoughts go through a thrifty Trustafarian's mind: "These sneakers look like they could have been draped over a power line!" "These coveralls are going to look so much more awesome on me than on that real mechanic—who, judging by these stains, probably killed some people. Cool." "Don't they teach you not to put knitwear on hangers in public schools? I'll take it."

Just as the world of fashion is always changing, so is the niche of recycled clothing. Designers step in to reimagine just what a piece of clothing can be, and this goes far beyond the previous arm warmer exercise. (If you want to make more arm warmers, feel free to do so now. Do it to all the sweaters in your home—not just yours.)

A little gem in New York is the store AuH2O, where khaki pants become ladies' tops and men's button-downs and T-shirts unite to become a single hybrid shirt. Trustafarians love this because it ups the ante for old clothes, and rarely are they talented or patient enough to sew anything themselves.

Five Rules of Trustafarian Fashion

1. Never let clothing show wealth.

2. Never wear something your parents bought you directly without cutting it up.

3. Dress for the job no one wants, not the job you stopped showing up for.

4. Never experiment with turtlenecks. They are like the Chinese finger trap of fashion. Once you stick your head in one of them, there is no pulling back from the shame.

5. If you have to buy something from Abercrombie & Fitch, Old Navy, Gap, L.L. Bean, American Eagle Outfitters, or from any store in a mall, use cash and burn all receipts.

UNDERGARMENTS
Nah.

THE SHOES
Unification across the entire spectrum of Trustafarians comes from a certain floppy footwear: sandals. Sandals instantly anchor a dreadlocked head and create an outfit out of any pieces in between. They bring a Trustafarian close to the earth and bring the tops of their feet close to the air. It is also a convenient way for them to distance themselves from family money, because an exposed toe conjures up images of poverty—unless it is due to an open-toed slingback number photographed on Victoria Beckham.

Some Trustafarians cannot be bothered with footwear. To them, life is a coal walk. Also, if a Trustafarian ever drops a coin, a guitar pick, a lime wedge, or something difficult to grab with fingers—not to mention the hassle of bending over—a bare foot is a great way to use the body's natural stickiness to pick up an object. All he/she needs to do is press down on the fallen object with pressure just strong enough to leave an impression and easily, within four or five tries, a dropped object is lifted up by the foot to a level where it can be reached by a hand.

An excellent way to still accessorize the foot without protecting or insulating it is by painting toenails or wearing an anklet.

Crocs are never worn by Trustafarians, as they are similarly not worn by anyone concerned with how they look. Also, they are notorious escalator hazards, and Trustafarians are notorious for daydreaming and losing track of what they should be doing when riding an escalator. This is also why Trustafarians double-knot their shoes.

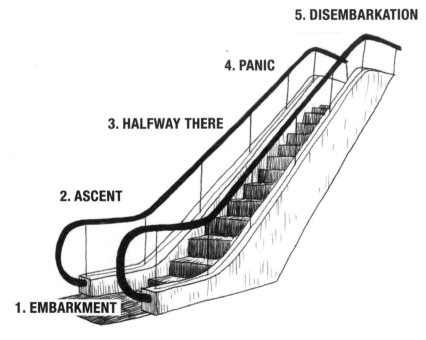

FIGURE 5.c. *The phases of an upward escalator ride and what goes through a Trustafarian's mind in each. Check out these steps in action the next time you are at an airport or subway station.*

Stage 1: Embarkment. I have to go upstairs to the R train.
Stage 2: Ascent. Zzzz.
Stage 3: Halfway There. Why are the walls moving?
Stage 4: Panic. Holy shit! Am I in a mall?
Stage 5: Disembarkation. More panic! Jump for your lives!

THE HAIR

It is a common experience. You are walking down the street and you pass by a Trustafarian, for this example, a female Impostafarian. She turns her nose up at you, and you think it means she feels superior to you. You are wrong. She knows she is better than you, but she is turning her nose up because her vegetarian diet has made her bones weak and her hair is so heavy it snaps her head back like a Pez dispenser under a greasy nine-year-old kid's palm.

> **dread** (drĕd) n.
> *Rastafarian:* an individual dreadlock
> *Parents of Trustafarians*: the feeling experienced when seeing a blossoming Trustafarian's hair

JAH'S DREADED CHILDREN

Dreadlocks are a favorite hairstyle of Trustafarians because of their association with Rastafarianism, the rejection of materialism, and proud black people on television. They ensure that any time POTs introduce their Trustafarian children to their friends, some sort of qualifier is necessary to explain why their child has fallen through the glass ceiling. Here are some common introductions:

- "This is Natalie. She's a creative soul."
- "This is Archie, but he has a black name now."
- "Annie couldn't make it. We're hosting Gungunno for the semester. She doesn't speak English."
- "This is Loki, and she grew her hair to spite me, so I am leaving her with you. I hate her."

For Trustafarians, dreads are a viral hairstyle. Research is not done into origins and meaning, but people who sport dreads carry an attitude that is strong, and they almost look like a lion! Lions are, of course, both strong and very African. Many Trustafarians are attracted to this unique show of power and dreadlocks become the way to achieve it.

Within the many thin pages of the Bible (which have also been used as rolling paper) there is a statement that says men should not cut their hair. As far as styles of never-cut-hair go, dreadlocks are one of the tidiest and certainly the most fashionable. Singer Crystal Gayle with her silky mega-mane may provide competition, but dreadlocks have geometry and architecture with which wispy floor-dragging locks cannot compete.

Considered in their bulky entirety, dreadlocks are stylish, God-friendly, symbolic of African pride and fierce safari animals, and are therefore the perfect Impostafarian hair.

There are three primary ways for Trustafarians to achieve dreadlocks. Here they are, explained in detail, so that if a Trustafarian friend ever asks you for hair advice, you can be informed and ready to answer/read aloud from this book.

Trusty Dreadlock Method #1: Home Schooled

This is the least common method of the three, but it is listed first to show the basics of dreadlockery. These steps are not meant to be followed exactly. The figuring out of how to make dreadlocks is a trial by fire, an initiation into the Impostafarians' world.

STEP 1: CALL UP A FRIEND WHO MIGHT KNOW SOMETHING ABOUT THEM Invite them over to dread your hair. Tell them it will take only a half-hour. This is not necessarily a lie; it is just a poor estimate of the time span required.

STEP 2: SECTION Using rubber bands, wire, or some sort of temporary binding device (not gum), divide your hair into sections that will become your dreadlocks. These sections will last as long as the dreads, so try to divide your individual hairs into groups where you think they will be happy and get along with each other.

Always overestimate how many final locks you would like to have. You and your friend will get tired, lose patience after awhile, and begin making bigger dreads to save time. Final count should be somewhere between 25 and 60, so plan for 200 if you need to.

STEP 3: BACKCOMB If you are familiar with the British comedian and somehow MTV Video Music Awards host Russell Brand, you know the macabre splendor of backcombing. The process is simple. Normally hair is combed from the root toward the tips. In backcombing, the direction is reversed. Work each section until it is a ragged mess.

STEP 4: WAX AND TWIRL There are some waxes made specifically for white people who want to turn their hair into a wild series of ropes. Those are probably the best options, though if you do not have the foresight to plan ahead, egg whites or glue sticks are workable substitutes. Roll the sections of hair between your hands or twirl them with your fingers.

It is also a good idea, as you are twirling your locks, to periodically tug on the hair and rip it. Of course, you will lose some hair, but the shorter strands' damaged ends help to "lock" the hair into its final shape. Also, the sound of hair ripping is unique and unforgettable.

STEP 5: BLOW-DRY Blow-drying will help the wax or wax substitute melt into the locks and remove bacteria-nutritive moisture from the hair.

STEP 6: FREAK OUT AND WONDER IF YOU MADE A HORRIBLE MISTAKE Now that you see yourself, it will start to sink in that the person you see in the mirror is the new you. It is usually shocking, and a tumult of emotion may overtake you. This is why you really need the friend—who is currently pissed that you made him waste a whole evening only to end up watching you bitch and cry—to comfort you and tell you that you look awesome.

Trusty Dreadlock Method #2: Pay

An easier but less-climactic way to get dreadlocks is by paying a salon artist to create them. Trustafarians enjoy this because it combines rapidity and spending their parents' money in a way their parents would not very much like.

STEP 1: PAY Give your salon artist $400.

STEP 2: BE PAMPERED Receive gentle scalp massage with grapefruit oil and a hair wash at the water temperature of your choosing. See what drinks are available. See what drinks are not available. Ask for those.

STEP 3: LET THE SALON ARTIST DO HIS/HER THING Wait four hours, and do not cry like a baby.

STEP 4: TIP Twenty-five dollars for every hour you sat in the salon is a reasonable amount. Remember, you could have done this at home and only sprung a buck for the glue stick.

Trusty Dreadlock Method #3: Neglect

This method is also very common.

STEP 1: NEGLECT YOUR HAIR In just a few years you will either have dreadlocks—or a dreadlock. A very common result of this method (and others, if the strands are not separated well enough) is the creation of a unidread. One head yields one dreadlock, and it is not very pretty. It may be useful in saving someone trapped in a narrow well.

TRUST FUN! | # Amateur Entomology!

Legend (due to far too many claims and sources to sort through) states that at the time of Bob Marley's death he had dozens of insects living inside his hair, many of which were, up until that point, undiscovered. Are the Marley Bugs really a new species? Scientists and tabloid readers can only speculate. Assume though, for the sake of this activity, that it is absolutely true. If you have a dreaded Trustafarian for a friend, use the opportunity to discover some new species of your own.

STEP 1: Wait until your Trustafarian is agreeable or unconscious.

STEP 2: Remove a lock. If you think this will be particularly noticeable, just examine it while it is still affixed to the Trustafarian's head.

STEP 3: Scavenger Hunt! See what sort of treasures are waiting to be discovered inside. Use a magnifying glass for small treasures, or just your eyes for obvious nesters, and see what is inside. If you have another friend with you, you may turn this into a contest. See who can find the most of these items:

❑ Insects
❑ Small mammals
❑ WWE action figures
❑ Ear buds (headphone pieces)
❑ Bottle caps
❑ Pretzels
❑ Concert tickets
❑ Car keys
❑ Ganja and/or related paraphernalia
❑ Twenty-nine-cent stamps
❑ Something borrowed

CONTINUED ON NEXT PAGE

STEP 4: Science! You or whoever won the scavenger hunt should gather up all the potentially new species of insect and small mammal and bring them to your local science center, sell them, name them after yourself if possible, and profit.

FIGURE 5.d. *What will you find?*

Upkeep

After becoming dreaded, there is an initial period of attention and care that must be paid to dreadlocks. Most hair, especially those types that are not particularly coarse, will need to be waxed every few days for several weeks. Salon appointments should be scheduled in advance for this.

Drying dreadlocks completely before applying the wax is a helpful way to avoid odors and non-hair growths. Many Trustafarians do not realize this or opt not to care. The resultant odor is reminiscent of the empty end of a crowded subway car or unattended gym equipment.

Other hair odors arise when Trustafarians try to help make their hair coarse by burning sections of it. Sometimes this is done accidentally. Trustafarians spend a lot of time near fire. As an intentional means to coarser hair, it is both noxious and dangerous, so it should be avoided.

After a while dreadlocks will become self-sustaining. The only thing to contend with will be the growth of new hair, which should just be waxed and twirled in as it shows up. This step is usually forgotten and the result is a garden of tiny wisps that break off from the rest of the hair and rise above the dreadlocks, creating a fuzzy effect, similar to when someone clamps onto the static electricity ball at the science museum.

Ornamentation

Dreadlocks mimic the texture of hemp jewelry. As such, they can be similarly decorated. Wooden beads are very common, adding an earthy touch with a sense that someone just got off the Black Pearl.

Metal bands (like strips of metal, not a music group) and repurposed earrings are also good ways to add a little pep to any set of drab locks.

Dreadlocks may also function as decorations on their own. Using two front strands to bind all of the other strands by tying a knot at the back of the head is very common and very fashionable.

Trustafarians should not feel limited in enhancing their locks. Encourage them to experiment with nontraditional items such as Christmas ornaments, fly-fishing lures (or anything that is used for fishing), wind chimes, plastic light-up chili peppers, and useful tools, like ratchets and pencils.

Those Trustafarians who are prone to forget things may also want to keep a spare house key up there.

TRUST FUN! | **More Fun with Trustafarian Hair!**

There are lots of exciting things to do with your Trustafarian's hair. Do not limit yourself to finding things that are already inside it. Put things in there as well. An excellent Trust Fun idea—and again, wait until your Trustafarian is agreeable or unconscious—is to hide a geocache inside.

If you are unfamiliar, geocaching is a typically outdoor, GPS-based treasure hunt and widely regarded as a lot of fun. Small containers are hidden

CONTINUED ON NEXT PAGE

---

all over the world and geocachers (those prone to partaking in geocaching) are given coordinates and clues to find them. There is a website that explains all of this.

> **NOTE:** Hiding a geocache in your friend's hair may go against the spirit of geocaching, and it could violate some laws, so use your judgment.

If you decide to proceed, set up the cache in a small film canister and place it in your Trustafarian's hair. Leave a tiny logbook and a golf pencil so that tourists and cache hunters can write their names and leave comments about their visit to your friend's head. Providing accurate coordinates may be tricky as your Trustafarian moves around, but you know your friend. It is likely that he/she only spends time in three or four different places. Choose one of those.

FIGURE 5.e. *In pursuit of the elusive Trustafarian*

The look of confusion on his/her face when some middle-aged hikers knock on the apartment door and ask to touch his/her hair will be priceless.

POST-DREADLOCKS

DAD: What the hell did you do to your hair!

JUNIOR: Relax. I'll comb it out tomorrow.

Dreadlocks are very much permanent, unlike a Japanese perm or a severe bob, there is no easy, eventual return. This is a fact many Impostafarians are unaware of when they choose this style. Sometimes the choice is impulsive. Sometimes it is just because a cool chick hairstylist offered a lot of money to get test dummies for her dreading techniques. Planning ahead is not a Trustafarian strong suit, but it does not matter, as the dreadlocks fit in well with the lifestyle.

Hardcore Impostafarians are likely to stick to their hair choice until death and see lock loss as a sign of turning away from Rastafarian ideas.

Celebrities who have axed their dreads and are now dead to Impostafarians:
- Busta Rhymes
- Eric Benét
- Lauryn Hill
- Lenny Kravitz
- That fast girl from *Heroes*, Brea Grant
- S. Epatha Merkerson

For most other Trustafarians, there will come a day when the dreadlocks must come to an end. The deciding factor could be anything:

- Chronic neck pain
- Trouble bubble gum
- Overfed, overhead seagull
- Whim
- Narrowly survived episode with chain link/tree/headboard

After the dreads are gone, Trustafarians will have a very difficult time readjusting to natural hair. Having been removed from standard grooming for so long, they have forgotten things that most people take for granted, like getting haircuts and combing or brushing. Hair just sits on the head as it grows out after being clipped at the roots to remove the dreads. Without being contorted into tubules, it has a tendency to drape about the head like a dead ferret. The newly shorn Trustafarians are so used to having their hair look weird and take care of itself that they often do not spot anything wrong with their hairstyle until it is pointed out by people they trust—other Trustafarians, who for the most part, do not notice either.

> The dead ferret style is a key way for people to identify Trustafarians who do not wear the telltale locks.

THE UNIVERSAL STYLE

This style takes its name from that crazy, only vaguely understood, questionably shaped, rapidly expanding, unbridled, and vast Universe that everyone and everything calls "home." This is a very natural hair choice that can be thought of as prestyle. For both men and women, hair grows quite long. It is very hippie-esque. Simple ponytails are common. Occasionally, a simple braid or two will be added out of boredom. Post-dreadlock styles generally evolve to fit this frizzy form. Trusta-

FIGURE 5.f. *Naturally awesome*

farians also usually have exceptionally thick hair. This most likely was a trait received from their successful parents, whose thick manes got them ahead in the business world. For the same reason, Trustafarians generally tend to be tall and have great skin. This tends to frustrate the pockmarked and balding middle-classers they pass on the street, as if those people did not have enough reasons to be jealous already.

Hair Inspiration: People Who Rock the Universal Style

Ozzy Osbourne, Helena Bonham Carter (who makes it work), Jessie Spano, 1970s *Saturday Night Live* cast members—except for Jane Curtin, who managed to find a comb.

THE COW CUD STYLE

A few short styles exist for Trustafarians. The cow cud style is great for both men and women who are constantly waking up for naps. This multidirectional and messy style gets its name because it looks like a cow has been sucking on it after having previously sucked on it and vomited.

FIGURE 5.g. *Raggedy awesome*

Hair Inspiration: People Who Rock the Cow Cud Style

Gary Busey, Tim Burton, Wolverine, Richie Sambora, Cosmo Kramer (and the rest of the *Seinfeld* core cast at one point or another)

TRUSTAFARIAN SPOTLIGHT ON

Julia Louis-Dreyfus

Yes, she is Elaine from *Seinfeld*, a *Saturday Night Live* staple of the early eighties (What can you do?), and *Old Christine*, which Trustafarians have never seen. This breaker of the *Seinfeld* curse is most well known for her acting and increasing sexiness with age. She is less well known for being the daughter of a French billionaire. This is what Trustafarians find exceptionally tolerable about her. Her massive wealth is in the shadow of the popular portions of her biography.

When a young Brohemian male looks to Paris Hilton, he thinks, "I'd tap that heiress if I had to." When he thinks of Louis-Dreyfus, he simply thinks, "funny milf." Her celebrity is almost completely devoid of family money. That is a Trustafarian dream.

She is a favorite of Fauxlanthropists, who often feel talented.

EIGHT-DOLLAR GUY CUT

Some little boys grow up with a steady rhythm of monthly trips to get their hair done—always the same style, always the same flavor lollipop after the cut. Change can be difficult for Trustafarians. Brohemians especially are likely to see no reason to break form from the serviceable do they have had for two or more decades. Other available hairstyles will often seem too ethnic, too vintage, or too metro, all of which would make

FIGURE 5.h. *Awesome enough*

them stand apart from their bros. The best choice for them is the $8 guy cut: short on top and progressively shorter as it travels down the cranium. Tapered and simple, this no thinker is a habit that gives Trustafarians' moms and dads at least one piece of evidence that they did some parenting. It also gives twenty-somethings a comforting reminder of the lollipop received from the shaky, liver-spotted hand of their childhood barber.

Hair Inspiration: People Who Rock the Eight-Dollar Guy Cut

Police officers, gym teachers, little league teams, Herman Munster, today's Mark Harmon

NEXT TO NOTHING

Anyone with hair clippers or a Flowbee can pull off this look. It follows the same reasoning as most Trustafarian styles. It is incredibly easy to deal with day to day. Once a week simply buzz your head (or have a friend do it,) and you are good to go!

FIGURE 5.i. *Rough and tough and awesome*

A hood is the most common accessory for head stubble. With drawstrings to hold in heat, hoods really do the job of hair, while also being part of a shirt.

Hair Inspiration: People Who Rock Next to Nothing

Vin Diesel, Sinéad O'Connor, Natalie Portman circa 2005, kiwifruit

Cosmetics

Au naturale is the makeup style of choice for Trustafarians, though some will stray and paint themselves. Many hipster men can often be found wearing eyeliner, but the Trustafarian males often do not see the point. It would only attract the wrong kind of attention, crushing the "Bro" in Brohemian and inviting ridicule to other Trustafarian types.

The ladies of the Trustafari have a bit more freedom. A Rasta color scheme in strategic areas can really give a white girl the edge she needs to claim her Impostafarian title. Gold, crimson, and viridian eye shadows applied boldly on the eyelids and swept up into the brow make any eye color seem less important than Rastafarian symbolism.

Fingernails and toenails are also blank canvases for these three colors. Impostafarian females can make a statement with each trip to the manicurist. They can even request a small lion be painted onto their middle fingers as well.

An expensive mani-pedi can easily go awry if those colors are out of order, so Trustafarians have come up with a couple of helpful ways to remember the order of green-yellow-red. The first is to think of a stoplight.

GREEN: you begin, and you go.
YELLOW: slow down.
RED: Stop, you are done.

Another way is by using the mnemonic "Gorgeous Young Rasta." The first initials of each word correlate to each color.

MAKEOVER BY MARY JANE

For those Trustafarian females who find those colors too gaudy for makeup or those mnemonics too difficult for memory, there is another Trustafarian makeup staple: hemp!

Hemp arises again in its usual glory to form beauty products. Most commonly found in lip products, e.g., lipsticks and lip balms, these are often difficult to find in stores, but may be easily purchased with express shipping options from the Internet. Many other beauty products have hemp oil infused into them. Is it because hemp oil makes a great long-lasting, no-smear makeup? Absolutely not. The reason is clear. The word *hemp* sells.

TRUSTAFARIAN MARKETING TROUBLE

Trustafarians are a puzzling consumer group. Advertisers and their agencies often neglect or avoid campaigns directed to them. It is clear that Trustafarians' buying power is unprecedented, but they are also a relatively small demographic. Ad executives focus on making products look sexy to millions of teenage girls, a demographic that they understand and can easily study/remold, rather than marketing to the mysterious Trustafarians. Here are the key issues faced by advertisers when considering a Trustafarian campaign:

- Trustafarians would never show up to a focus group, no matter how much you paid them. They just do not want that money.
- There is an inverse ratio of corporate presence to Trustafarian interest. Trustafarians consider advertising to be for the masses, which they of course do not consider themselves a part of.
- Ad execs either do not understand or are uncomfortable with what Trustafarians find to be sexy.

- Trustafarians are hard to reach. Successful advertising through traditional media would require that Trustafarians pay attention to the TV, actually read a magazine, listen to ad-supported radio, or care what a billboard says. Online banner ads just piss them off, which leaves strategic viral campaigning as the only viable but difficult option.
- Teen idols are easily coaxed into licensing their names and images to products. Trustafarian idols are scary.

The best way to reel in the Trustafarian consumer and other ganjaphiles is by adding hemp in any way possible to a product. It is an undisputedly versatile plant, but hemp-infused tanning lotion would not be made if it were not for the reason that hemp helps it sell. Hemp is the Trustafarian weak spot. Like Mac users who assume no virus or worm will ever grace their computers because they think villainous programmers only target PCs, Trustafarians are completely off guard when a simple and old-school trick is played on them. As more and more advertisers catch on, do not be surprised to see hemp popsicles and hemp staplers on store shelves soon.

Hemp mayonnaise is a real thing!

Tattoos

Tattoos are an easy step toward rebellion and are therefore embraced by many Trustafarians. Some even deem themselves qualified enough to give tattoos to others at home.

The tattoo's location will depend on the motivation for getting it. If a Trustafarian wants to show a parent that he/she hates them or can do anything he/she pleases, hands, middle fingers, lower legs, necks, and faces are all excellent locations.

For the Trustafarians who want to rebel privately and not have Mom and Dad stop paying them to exist, shoulders, lower backs, hips, and biceps are all appropriate. The tattoos themselves can be anything.

TOP TRUSTAFARIAN TATTOO DESIGNS

Impostafarians
- Marijuana leaf
- Misunderstood reggae lyrics
- Mating lizards/insects/humans

Fauxlanthropists
- Marijuana leaf
- Peace/anarchy signs
- The starting dot to something much more painful

Brohemians
- Marijuana leaf
- Alf, a Snork, Batman, anything memorable from childhood that seems cool at the time
- Discolored patch where friend-ridiculed tattoo used to be

Diddlysquatters
- Marijuana leaf
- An insignificant pet's face with the birth and death dates approximated
- "I fucked your mom!"

Living Furs

Just as a bong or a car can be a status symbol, so can a small mammal, large reptile, or enormous bird. Top choices are animals that require a pool or an aviary. If an animal sleeps in a terrarium, it is acceptable as long as it is able to spend copious amounts of time worn like a boa, over the shoulders, or like a clutch, held in the hand. For this reason, fish are not options—unless of course they are fighting fish and they provide a spectator sport.

Why would a Trustafarian settle for a housecat when they can purchase the offspring of one that mated with a leopard? Exclusive hybrid pets from companies like Lifestyle Pets offer a way for Trustafarians to show their wealth but in a way that is undeniably magnificent. That little pussy is going to dominate any city pet park he enters. The lion-tiger hybrid, the liger, would be a choice pet except for its massive size, which makes its parents seem tiny. These animals are far more of a hassle than they are a novelty. As a result, you only see them in the bizarre research facilities where they are birthed and put on display.

Ermines, prairie dogs, meerkats, and golden lion marmosets also make great display pets. Their ability to be content in a confined space for long periods of time is limited, but Trustafarians will probably tire of their pets first.

Poodles are not often chosen as canine companions due to their prim and prissy image, but poodle hybrids are very common, as their hybrid names come with jokes already built into them (maltipoos, cockapoos, bossi-poos, and cavapoos). Some people attribute the success of these hybrids to the poodles' intelligent nature. Most Trustafarians will disagree. It is all about the naming convention.

Raptors make impressive pets, but the legality can be tricky. Oftentimes people will have to prove themselves as professional falconers, using the birds to hunt. Arguably, a Trustafarian using them as hunters is more dangerous than using them to play fetch. Either way, obtaining a vicious and intelligent bird as a pet increases a Trustafarians formidability exponentially.

Trustafarians are usually very clever with pet names—and if not clever, then just hilarious. Pets will sometimes be given cute child names to fill an emotional void. These include "Sarah," "Jane," and "Nancy." Other times, ironic nomenclature will be the goal, like "Bowser" for a kitten or "Snuggles" for an abrasive water dragon. The names can be quite long, like "Captain

Justice, Emotional Billionaire: A Lady Hawk," or short and to the point, like "Bitch." Pets will often be bought just to give them names.

> The original motivation for the phrase "elephant in the room" is unclear, but a safe bet is that the speaker knew a Trustafarian pet lover. Be careful using this phrase around excitable Trustafarians, or your next party may be a bit cramped.

You now know everything it takes to be a Trustafarian for your next costume party. Heirasites, you now know everything you need to know about Trustafarian fashion to pass in daily life. You just need a few staples and probably a few staples to hold them together. Also, having one of those Mwanza flat-headed rock agamas (the lizards that looks like Spider-Man) could not hurt.

Black and White

This Thick Line Between Trustafarians and Rastafarians Finally Explained!

Melanin is a funny thing, coloring eyes and skin and making for easy—though unfair—social grouping. Desire is also a funny thing. Everyone seems to want what he/she cannot have. In the Impostafarians' case, they want it all, and they probably already have most of it—except for one thing. They are not black.

Oh, they try very hard though, keeping many Rastafarian Internet startups afloat. Rasta gear, primarily knitwear and beadwork, go a long way in helping an Impostafarian stand out from other racial interlopers, and sometimes—but not too often—it does help.

While other Trustafarian types may not seek integration, they generally live harmoniously alongside Rastafarians in large or laid-back cities. Fauxlanthropists identify Rastafarian ideals of peace, vegetarianism, and the shunning of wealth as ideals they would love to have for themselves. Brohemians and Diddlysquatters enjoy having Rastafarians around because they assume it will lead them to weed.

The Journey

How Impostafarianism begins is much like a star. A budding Trustafarian is trapped in a swirling cloud of confusion, doomed to collapse and explode, reborn. Maybe a young girl decides her parents do not care for her and she needs some new sense of community. Maybe a young boy is losing his faith. The selling points of a previous church, perhaps Catholic, with its shared wine goblets, stale wafers, and mandatory attendance at weekly religious classes while friends of the attendee are off discovering a new God in marijuana, may lose their gravity compared to an edgy new religious discovery where God and cannabis are intertwined for a deluge of enlightenment.

TIPS FOR HELPING YOUR IMPOSTAFARIAN MOVE TOWARD LEGITIMACY

1. Have him/her seek Rastafarian mentors while still young. There is a definite age cap for looking cute while asking a Rastafarian if you could join his/her religion. The age limit may vary from person to person, but it is definitely under twenty-five.

2. Do not use the topic of ganja to get a conversation going. Actual narcs learn this the first day of class.

3. An offering of actual ganja might not be legal, but it also is not the worst idea. Sharing is caring. Prove legitimate interest from the onset.

4. A lot of major cities have big public parks where Rastafarians like to hang out. Remember that not all people with dreadlocks are Rastafarians. Look for red, green, and yellow. It may be stereotyping, but any casting director will tell you that typing out goes a long way for efficiency.

5. While in the park, remember that Rastafarians may be suspicious of an overly eager rich white kid asking them personal questions. If an overly eager man with dreadlocks cannot wait to share information with you in the woods off a bike path, be cautious. One might learn more about hand-job etiquette. Follow trails where you smell some herb, not ones marked with condom wrappers.

There is weed, there is music, there is a rejection of the material goods worshiped by Mom and Dad, but among many, there is a qualifier. To be a Rastafarian, many Traditional Rastafarians say, one must be black, or a passable, dark Caribbean Latino.

An Impostafarian in the making wonders, "What is this amazing, laid-back brotherhood among men?" It is not always easy to find out. A quick visit to Wikipedia provides a launching point and is quite possibly the only research done by many Impostafarians before storming down to the dinner table, knocking off some plates and forks to get attention, and proclaiming, "I am a Rastafarian!" It is a bold, though relatively meaningless, first step.

True(ish) Colors

It is a real test of Impostafarian perseverance, going against melanin, basic principles of light reflection, and popular opinion. An Impostafarian might identify as a black person trapped inside a white person's body. Any surgical options to correct such an occurrence would undoubtedly stir up decades of oppressive popular entertainment, with burnt cork used to darken the faces of the minstrel show.

Have a little sympathy for the Impostafarians in your life. The next stage of their journey after coming out is a long and possibly endless plateau of rejection and intolerance. If they are your children, give them interracial hugs and wish them the best. If they are your friends, count them among your black friends, for their sake. If they are not particularly dear to you, just ignore them. They are relatively harmless.

NONVIABLE OPTIONS FOR IMPOSTAFARIAN RACIAL TRANSITIONING

Extreme Bronzer: gives blotchy/carotenemic coloration

Melanin injections: do not work; needle-caused ouchies

Blackface: likely to receive punches in exaggerated lips

Black robot proxy: too expensive; short battery life or power cord entanglement

Hit the lights and Do Eddie Murphy impression: Murphy still not forgiven for what he did to Scary Spice

---

The dream of becoming a fully actualized, black Rastafarian more frequently ends incompletely than it does happily. While being black is not necessarily absolute, it is restricted. President Barack Obama, Halle Berry, and Tiger Woods all get to claim it, but at the same time white, out-of-Africa emigrants from tens of thousands of years ago do not qualify. Everything in between is a huge gray area. Generally, there needs to be some strong melanin being expressed. Trace or ancient amounts of African ancestry are often not enough to qualify as black in modern times.

A Trustafarian may never be accepted, but that does not mean he/she cannot practice his/her beliefs in private—or in public, just away from the Rastafarians, who he/she finds intimidating. For a Trustafarian that has never felt a need to prove anything to anyone, this situation is still palatable.

While many Rastafarians will see skin tone as an unnecessary divider among people, others believe Jah separated people by skin for a reason. These competing notions are often too heavy for a Trustafarian to entertain.

VIABLE OPTIONS* FOR IMPOSTAFARIAN RACIAL TRANSITIONING

- **Adopt an African baby:** Someone has to supervise the kid while he learns about his African roots. Be sure to request a black child, as Africa is a mix of many skin tones.
- **Be More Black Than a Black Friend Who Is Not Particularly Black:** MIT grad students and people who like *Sex and the City* are excellent candidates.
- **Full Body Cast:** It may be deceitful, but if no one knows what's under those bandages, race is just waiting to be claimed. Also, the person in the cast is just waiting to be wheeled around.
- **Tanning Salon Lie-In:** This is a nonviolent protest modeled right after the Civil Rights Movement. A Trustafarian simply refuses to leave an active tanning bed until he/she is accepted as black—or dead, which is a legitimate cause for concern with this plan. Though not recommended for health reasons, this option is always well done.

lesser failures

Reasons They Might Think They Are Black

No one else would think they are black. Why do Impostafarians get such a notion?

- They listen to reggae, like some black people do.
- They were told they could be anything they wanted. This is the first thing they wanted. It must be possible.
- They saw all of the *Fast & Furious* movies in the theater.
- They have an apartment in the "black part of town."
- They voted Democrat—at least once.
- They once spoke to a gang member of possible African heritage.
- They keep the TV on for *Showtime at the Apollo*.
- They would like to see someone else try and do the weather as good as Roker.
- They directed a student production of *The Wiz*.
- They have an active profile at BlackPlanet.com and at least one black friend on the site.

Everyone else besides the Impostafarians is pretty much agreed that the Impostafarians are decidedly not black, but that is not to say that they cannot be Rasta.

HELP THE IMPOSTAFARIANS IN YOUR LIFE

Do them a favor. If they are successful in ingratiating themselves into the Rastafarian movement, congratulate them, but remind them that this is their only accomplishment. They have not and will never achieve being black. The more they are reminded the less likely they will be to cause horrific and awkward moments for you over the course of your relationship.

Insensitivity

You might be thinking that being an Impostafarian could be pretty offensive to black people and Rastafarians. Yes. A lot of times though, the Impostafarians will just be ignored. In the event that an Impostafarian does take that one step too far, Hallmark has an entire line of Mahogany cards that are very appropriate for black people and backed by some degree of market research. There are Mahogany cards for weddings, Kwanzaa, and most importantly for Trustafarians, sympathy. They also have cards with sound that play *Rapper's Delight* by Sugar Hill Gang and *I'm Every Woman* by Chaka Kahn. It is very fortunate that when Impostafarians put their feet in their mouths, they have these cards to speak and sing for them.

TRUST FUN! | ## Making the Best of Your Trustafarian's Racial Confusion

You know that your Trustafarian does not actually think that his skin is particularly dark. He/she has eyes and they do work. Even the colorblind can still note contrast. They may be under the assumption that their mindset or their relation to the world is equal to a black person's, and this can lead you into all sorts of awkward situations. Such occasions include poorly chosen gangster rap karaoke and inviting a predominantly black bar crowd to "kiss [one's] black ass!"

Your Trustafarian will not easily be dissuaded from creating these social faux pas. To keep your relationship relatively positive, you can use his/her racial confusion to your benefit.

- Get a free basketball hoop. As a famous title suggests, if they are black, they can jump. Make it a challenge and pick up some swag.

CONTINUED ON NEXT PAGE

- Get a free trip to Africa. Tell your Trustafarian you would love to accompany him/her on a trip to explore his/her roots . . . if you only had that money.
- Get a free trip to Chicago to see Oprah.
- More free stuff! Go through your Trustafarian's belongings and pick out things you like. Bring them to your Trustafarian's attention and say, "It is so white of you to own this _____." And then say "hello" to your new possessions.

Due largely to inferred—but unintentional—insults from Impostafarians, Fauxlanthropists tend to be the Trustafarian group with the highest number of black friends who actually like them. With their tangential involvement with art and charity, they tend to come across as like-minded people of all races. Brohemians still have their white college and prep school friends, though they may have picked up an African American, African Brit, or African African along the way. Diddlysquatters are probably lacking in friends but could easily have some close acquaintances who are white, black, green, or cyan. There is no social science that can fathom their networking.

irie (ī´rē) adv./adj.
Rastafarian: filled with positive emotion, all right
Trustafarian: uncomfortable and frightening (see "eerie" in English dictionaries)

Success, Mon!

With determination and likely multiple attempts to find his/her niche, an Impostafarian may find an opportunity to join the ranks of the true Rastafarians. An Impostafarian may reach this point after a long struggle and wonder, "What the crap did I just do?"

Adopting new religious beliefs is a serious step for anyone to take. Trustafarians will often run headlong into new situations without questioning their motivations. An Impostafarian should ask, "Do I believe in Jah?"

Casual participants without unshakable beliefs exist in many (if not all) religions. If Impostafarians finally find their opening, a welcoming group of active and accepting Rastafarians, and realize they have been faking it, they have nothing to fall back on. A shotta (Jamaican gangster) without a god is still a shotta, still Jamaican, and still part of that Impostafarian ideal. An Impostafarian without a god is just a rich white kid (possibly Asian).

JAH RULE

Faith may be a foreign concept to Trustafarians, who are often raised in households where money and aggressive investment are Jah. Trustafarians have already forsaken that almighty, so there is usually little problem eschewing other deities.

Impostafarians have pursued an ideal for themselves but perhaps not fully grasped the spiritual gravity of what they desire. They may have grown entangled in a dreamlike state where dancing dreadlocks beckon them like an index finger slowly curling and uncurling to summon them to unknown happiness. Dancing along a dizzying cloud of ganja's powerful perfume, their sky is ruby, gold, and emerald. A tremendous lion, like that one from *Narnia*, says hello, and then in a flash it all disappears. A Trustafarian awakes, holding an open Bible in a small meeting hall with folding chairs somewhere in Brooklyn, but nowhere near the Manhatten or a familiar subway group. It is the moment of enlightenment for the Trustafarian: Jah is essential. If the Trustafarian accepts Jah into his/her life, the Trustafarian's body is now a temple, and worshiping can be done right from his/her pasty skin.

If the Trustafarian cannot come to believe in Jah, then it is time to quietly back away, call a car service, and re-evaluate. A Rastafarian from Impostafarian beginnings can always return to his/her Impostafarian roots, but generally there is a hollowness that accompanies such a transition.

Trustafarians are not normally ones to learn things from their experiences. This is very true here as well. Generally they just find further proof that the world does not have a convenient home for them and that they must continue to seek their own way—a way that is pretty awesome but too frequently misunderstood.

> **man or mon** (măn or mŏn) n.
> *Rastafarian*: an individual male human
> *Trustafarian*: used to terminate any statement, command, exclamation, or question with an authentic Jamaican flair: *Take a number mon. Is this seat taken mon? Doesn't it suck what they did to Conan, mon?*

Impostafarian Transitions

IMPOSTAFARIAN DESIGNATED RASTAFARIAN

Spirituality has taken hold of the Trustafarian. Life's biggest hassles will now be convincing people of his/her legitimacy and questioning that Protestant certainty that Mom was going to hell.

IMPOSTAFARIAN DESIGNATED FAUXLANTHROPIST

After discovering that religion or spirituality requires belief in things that cannot be seen, a Trustafarian decides to spend time warning other Impostafarians of the expected responsibilities that come with the Rastafarian ideology. Life's biggest hassles will now be coping with Impostafarians who are as stubborn as he/she used to be and dropping the affected Jamaican accent.

IMPOSTAFARIAN DESIGNATED DIDDLYSQUATTER

The Impostafarian is keeping his/her Rasta style, but has lost all motivation for the time being. Life's biggest hassles will now be getting up in the morning and tying shoes.

IMPOSTAFARIAN DESIGNATED BROHEMIAN

Possibly involving a haircut, this reclassification involves a group of Diddlysquatters nee Impostafarians banding together to "bro it up." Life's biggest hassles are negligible with compatriots.

IMPOSTAFARIAN DESIGNATED IMPOSTAFARIAN

An Impostafarian has learned absolutely nothing and is just going to try again to be a Rastafarian. Their determination is lauded, but their comprehension skills are called into question.

Never Too Rich to Raid
a Fridge, Bitch!

For most people, abiding by a truly healthy, humane, and environmentally responsible diet comes with a price tag that makes ethical eating more of a delusion than a tangible reality. Trustafarians have never been bothered by something as trivial as a price tag. Any fad diet is up for grabs and within their means.

Hemp Returns (Again!)

Was there any doubt? There was none in the minds of faithful Trustafarians. This amazing plant can also be eaten in a way that causes neither a high or mellowing—just nutrition. The seeds can be eaten or can even be turned into milk, just like almonds, soybeans, and rice. Hemp oil is also available. Hemp seed nuts make a fantastic salad addition. If you ever find yourself tasked with preparing a meal in a Trustafarian kitchen, you may find cooking without this every-plant to be impossible.

FIGURE 7.a. *HEMP: "I'm back, bitches!"*

Hemp smoothies are just waiting to be blended, and hemp nog is right around the next holiday

corner. As a very important rule, remember to always ask your Trustafarian what ingredients are in the food you are about to eat or the drink you are about to drink. After you are assured your edibles and potables are perfectly normal, double check, possibly including a wink to help the Trustafarian recall any special ingredients he/she may have included.

As was mentioned in the chapter devoted to Ganja (Chapter 4), the more chemically active varieties of the hemp plant can also be used in many ways in the kitchen (and the bedroom, hallway, bathroom, or stairwell).

> **ital** (ĭ´tăl) n.
> *Rastafarian*: vital food, pure and natural, generally excluding meat, blood, alcohol, and drugs (as ganja is more of an herb)
> *Trustafarian*: slanty letters

Veganism

Many Trustafarians opt for vegan diets as an easy way to denote that they are more serious about their diet than simple vegetarians. The Trustafarian vegans will become scornful when they see someone eat a chicken nugget. They

FIGURE 7.b. *These fine-food products all appear in a Trustafarian vegan's diet.*

will make a point to draw attention to their entrée salad. They will demand that their food is prepared first on a grill before any vulgar meat is placed upon it. They will then often follow their vegan meal with a tasty scoop of ice cream. (The totality of vegan rules does not apply to the Trustafarian, much like the totality of all rules.)

Commercial Diet Plans

Female Trustafarians especially feel the need to eat right. Ever since childhood, their moms have been checking to see if they have a flat stomach. Men may also choose to diet just because they are bored and the commercials make diet food look fun and easy. Not everyone may be able to afford Jenny Craig's Premium Success Plan and The Martha's Vineyard Diet Detox, but they present no trouble for the Trustafarians. Those of you who have to wait for Healthy Choice meals to go on sale before buying them may find little solace knowing the Trustafarians can buy them at any time and eat six or seven during a single sitting.

Diets may last anywhere from one to three and a half days. Anything that involves a meeting or a private consultation is doomed for termination even before that first bite of frozen food is taken.

Gluten Intolerance Diet

Not very many people have a gluten intolerance, but a Trustafarian just might affect one. The gluten-intolerant never gain weight, which is incentive enough on its own. They also eat expensive bread from that special section in grocery stores. To the Trustafarians, this is clearly a luxury item, disguised as regular sliced bread. Being pricey and somewhat exclusive, the gluten intolerance diet is perfect for all Trustafarians.

Not Eating

A hunger strike is a particularly strong way for the child of a rich person to send a message. When poorer people hunger strike, there is a question as to whether or not they are just living within their means. The more socially conscious Fauxlanthropists know to take advantage of the situation. Losing weight never felt so good, and the way their strike will be celebrated afterward with a congratulatory feast gives Trustafarians a temporary sense of purpose.

Water Diet

After three months of living in a city and going to every restaurant at least twice, Trustafarians may get to the point where they are just too zonked to go out for more food. If they have neglected to pick up delivery menus and are unsure how to access the Internet through their new smart phone, Trustafarians may turn to the only sustenance on hand: water, fresh from the tap. As a crunchy, solid alternative, ice may be substituted.

Leisure Groceries

Trustafarians who live close to Mom and Dad will usually just walk home when they feel like a meal. This is done in the hopes that Mom and Dad are not there during the visit. Mom will usually have purchased a special treat for her child to find both as a display of love and as an attempt to distract the child from the food she bought for herself.

When confronted with either having to interact with parents or find food elsewhere, the Trustafarian will opt for a meal with friends. Friends have refrigerators too.

There are several reasons why a Trustafarian would not be able to go to an actual grocery store. These include house arrest, that pesky *No Shirt, No Shoes, No Service* rule, and lack of want. A variety of services cater to Trustafarians for these very circumstances. Those lucky enough to live in the New York metropolitan area can use their parents' credit cards to order from FreshDirect. Other similar services include Peapod, Netgrocer, and some guy with a van. The van guy will probably only take cash, but he will probably deliver substances that could not legally be sold at Stop & Shop or Publix. With plenty of available options, as long as the Trustafarian is not too stoned to answer the door or accurately type a credit card number, healthful and tasty treats are just a web form submission away—except for the guy with the van, who uses a beeper.

THE (IN)COMPLETE TRUSTAFARIAN FRIDGE

There are a few staples that every Trustafarian refrigerator contains:

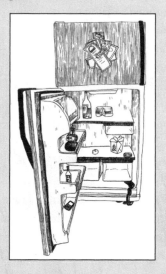

- Magnetic bottle opener
- Take-out menus
- Take-out
- White wine
- Limes
- Cheese
- Hot sauce
- Local restaurant guide
- Restaurant leftovers
- Antioxidant rich juice
- Ready-to-eat macrobiotic Peking duck
- Mystery residue

Cooking à la Trust Fund

To many Trustafarians, a stovetop is just added counter space. Ovens are added storage and the broiler drawer is just a place to put extra towels. If you live in the same building as a Trustafarian and are woken up to fire engine sirens at 3:00 A.M., it is because one of these storage solutions has caught fire. The best response would be to go stand out on the street in your bathrobe, because there is nothing else you can do, unless being severely burned seems enticing.

FIGURE 7.c. *Trustafarian Davis L. Pierre's fourth time attempting to bake a cake, fourth time forgetting he started, and fourth time he will have to move*

Broiled towels excluded, Trustafarians make the most use of one special piece of kitchen equipment: the microwave. All of those diet program meals heat up nearly satisfactorily in the microwave. Many Trustafarians do not have much experience cooking for themselves. The microwave presents an excellent entryway for them into the world of culinary arts.

FIGURE 7. d. *A place of comfort in a world of big and scary appliances*

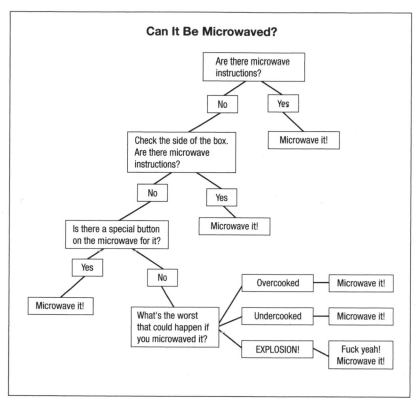

FIGURE 7.e. *The common thought process used to determine cooking method among inexperienced chefs like the Trustafarians*

If a Trustafarian is preparing a meal for you, expect surprising results. The bottle of wine that you brought over might just count as an entire meal, or there are always restaurants.

CHAPTER 8

Arts and Entertainment

Trivial Pursuit as a Hobby

This is the section of the handbook where you are eagerly waiting to hear about the cool, unique niche interests of the Trustafarians with which you are completely unfamiliar.

The only real problem with that is that Trustafarians enjoy the same crap as everyone else; they just oftentimes will not admit it. Sharing income sources with gentry threatens their cultural status enough. Admitting to shared interests could destroy their identities. They will readily admit to liking Marley and dumpster diving, but only because they play to the Trustafarian image. Eating at Olive Garden, reading PerezHilton.com, and listening to John Mayer will all be concealed or denied, but they are not uncommon pastimes.

This section of The Trustafarian Handbook will instead focus on a few particular Trustafarian trends and explore, by way of compiled social networking examples, commonalities among the Trustafarians groups.

Social Networking Sample: **Impostafarian**

Jennifer Lee Cabot-Royale is off to talk to the 'farians in the park! Cell.

Info

Basic Information _____

Name: Jennifer Lee Cabot-Royale
Religious Views: Rasta
Political Views: Politricks

Likes and Interests _____

Favorite Music: Marley (One Love!!!), Peter Tosh, Roots, Matisyahu, Kanye, Wyclef Jean, Al Green, Damian Marley, Ziggy Marley, anything but country
Favorite Movies: Shottaz, Shawshank Redemption, Precious, Rushmore, Hancock, Night of the Living Dead, Fight Club, Do the Right Thing, Jungle Fever
Favorite TV Shows: Real Housewives of Atlanta, The Cleveland Show, Harlem Heights
Favorite Books: I don't really read but I read some of the kebra negast

Contact Information _____

AIM Screen Name: GanjaMiss614

Games Trustafarians Play

Though some cannot find a limit, there is only so long most Trustafarians can go on complaining about their parents in a social setting. The hurt of that ensuing silence and the inability to show emotional weakness in front of friends necessitate that Trustafarians distract themselves.

Video games are an excellent redirection of focus, and a favorite of nearly all Trustafarians because 1) the Trustafarians generally have enormous television sets and 2) slightly harsh realities can be escaped. For Trustafarians, the greatest game to ever be hastily inserted into a for-no-reason-gift Wii is *The Beatles: Rock Band*. For the first time, "Dear Prudence" has become playable by a guitarist with zero talent. This game prompts Trustafarians' parents to briefly assume they have something in common with their children—Beatle love—but Trustafarians will not allow them to play, unless of course a Trustafarian is short a second guitarist, in which case game play goes something like this:

TRUSTAFARIAN: Green! Green, Dad—Christ! Hit Green! No, Green! Oh my fuck—Green! It's just green! No, now it's red. Why would you—you're holding it wrong. Stop. Just put it down. God!

Never has there been so much intergenerational bonding! Never has Dad smashed so many fake guitars!

> *Rock Band* and *Guitar Hero* were really the first games to win over the majority of female Trustafarians, who now request it be played at every social (or antisocial) gathering.

Social Networking Sample: **Fauxlanthropist**

Reagan Farrah Turner cookin' sum curry veggie chicken leftover from last night trip to India House with the reformed convicts

---

Info

Basic Information ────────────────────────────────

Name: Reagan Farrah Turner
Religious Views: pastafarian
Political Views: really really really leftish

Likes and Interests ──────────────────────────────

Favorite Music: Handel, Bach, Dylan, Joplin, Hendrix, Marley, Annie Lennox, Phish, Beatles, Wu-Tang, Jamiroquai, DMB, anything except country
Favorite Movies: Rushmore, 16 Candles, Stranger than Fiction, Fight Club, Mommie Dearest, Y Tu Mama Tambien, Empire Records, so many lol
Favorite TV Shows: I don't watch TV. CSpan2, CNN, HGTV
Favorite Books: Middlesex, The Kite Runner, Harry Potter, lol so many. . . .
I want to have one of those giant libraries with a swinging ladder a la Beauty and the Beast

Contact Information ──────────────────────────────

AIM Screen Name: Kiss4artgirl

TRUSTAFARIAN SPOTLIGHT ON
Dhani Harrison

Dhani Harrison (George's son) worked in a vague capacity getting *The Beatles: Rock Band* made, and he did get it made, after having some sort of meetings with his dad's friends. With a large inheritance, Harrison is prime Trustafarian material, but did he manifest Trustafarian tendencies?

He did go to Brown, which resulted in a video game career, and he did play guitar for the Wu-Tang Clan's quasi-cover of *While My Guitar Gently Weeps*, which added hundreds of lyrics George would have never dreamed up or said in public. As of now, he is indeed a Trustafarian. The only way he can louse it up is by continuing to hone his musical craft and being successful in his own right.

Aside from music simulation, video games that simulate drag racing and going on various rampages, such as the *Grand Theft Auto* series, also draw in the Trustafarians, particularly males, who are often just home from crashing their hybrid Prius into something or stealing their dad's car.

OLD SCHOOL GAMING

Not all Trustafarian games are of the video variety. There are many lower-tech options. Throwing things off of things onto things has always been an enjoyed pastime. Of course, there are Hacky Sack and Frisbee sports, but often times they may seem dreadfully active. Board games offer a nice indoor alternative—though the board will rarely be used. Instead, the *Trivial Pursuit* card boxes will be distributed to Trustafarians on neighboring couches. Between sighs, questions will be read and answered, for no points. If a question is answered incorrectly, the response from the asker will be a simple "no," with no further explanation. This goes on for weeks. The Sports & Leisure category is never chosen, but most Trustafarians can hold their own in the others—which may or may not have to do with the fact that they have been through each of the decks twelve times.

Games Trustafarians Will Not Play

MONOPOLY: They ardently avoid dealing with finances and property in real life, so why would they want to do it in a game?

LIFE/THE GAME OF LIFE: For Trust-afarians, this is just a nightmare.

YAHTZEE: It is just dice, there is math, and it is boring.

DOMINOES: Nothing topples.

CHESS: Why does the white man always get to move first?

FIGURE 8.a. *Racist!*

Boys and Bobs

Every boy loves a Bob. As you encounter Trustafarian males, this will become apparent very quickly. Bob Marley, strumming his ska and reggae, is the reigning king of Trustafarians. However, some Trustafarians may be uncomfortable with the pulsing offbeats or the connoted spirituality that accompanies Marley's participation in the Rastafari movement. Enter then, a second Bob: Bob Dylan. Dylan's use of song to comment on societal shortcomings sings to Trustafarians, who just hate the way the world is—outwardly. Inwardly, they do not want any one else's situation if it involves money loss.

Marley gets the Impostafarians, Dylan gets many of the Fauxlanthropists, and they split the remaining Trustafarian groups.

Social Networking Sample: **Brohemian**

Brayden Hayden Bloomfield who's gonna help me drink this leftover beer, bring more?

Info

Basic Information _____

Name: Brayden Hayden Bloomfield
Religious Views: laughing
Political Views: moderate

Likes and Interests _____

Favorite Music: Phish! Grateful Dead, Dylan, Strokes, Killers, anything, even some country but not a lot of country
Favorite Movies: Borat, Clerks, Rushmore, Office Space, Star Wars (all!), Rocky, check me out on youtube
Favorite TV Shows: Scrubs, Robot Chicken, Family Guy, Fraggle Rock
Favorite Books: not a reader

Contact Information _____

AIM Screen Name: Trip77SF

Another Bob of note is Bob Saget. It is not his stints on *Full House* or *America's Funniest Home Videos* (*AFV*) that endear him to the Trustafarians. It is his appearance in *The Aristocrats*, where he showed he was just as salacious and smutty as the other comedians—if not tremendously more. Knowing that, reruns of *Full House* and *AFV* suddenly become enjoyable.

Laughter is the best drug for forgetting your life situation for four to eight seconds. In addition to Bob Saget, these are some of the folks who sometimes manage to get a Trustafarian to crack a smile.

1. **Mitch Hedberg (resting in peace):** He did all those drugs that Trustafarians would love to honestly admit doing.

2. **Dave Chappelle:** *Chappelle's Show* was a Trustafarian favorite for touching on cable-appropriate race issues and having sketches that were actually funny.

3. **Demetri Martin:** He reminds them of Andy Samberg, who would have this spot on the list, had he not made fun of the Trustafari on *Saturday Night Live*.

4. Okay—**Andy Samberg:** Trustafarians put their "Dick in a Box" all the time, but they will only acknowledge Samberg when paired with Timberlake, whose music they do not know but whose comedy they appreciate.

Many people wonder if the Trustafari enjoy Dane Cook. The guys almost never enjoy him. He reminds them of people who were assholes in prep school. The ladies sometimes enjoy him, because he reminds them of the assholes they used to sleep with in prep school. Unfortunately, they enjoyed it.

Trustafarians also like Whoopi Goldberg because she has those dreadlocks and *Sister Act 2: Back in the Habit* made them feel good.

SpongeBob SquarePants is another—though very difficult to explain—Bob of Trustafarians. It is not uncommon to see a Trustafarian's social networking page adorned with an image of the anthropomorphic sea dweller, or his starfish friend. If you go looking, there is an excellent chance you will run across his questionably clever parodies, "SpongeBob SpliffPants" and "StonedBob HempPants."

Perhaps it is a desire to transform his pineapple home into a bong—it already has a chimney mouthpiece. Perhaps it is just a reminder of Trustafarians' dependent childlike state, and they refuse to let it go. Whatever the reason, this briny cartoon is a Trustafarian favorite.

Social Networking Sample: **Diddlysquatter**

Philip Arthur Walker IV is going to bed after 5 hours of being awake

---

Info

Basic Information ——————————————————————————

Name: Philip Arthur Walker IV
Religious Views: anti
Political Views: anti

Likes and Interests —————————————————————————

Favorite Music: phish marley music
Favorite Movies: v for vendetta, rushmore, tremors, donnie darko, fight club, movies
Favorite TV Shows: porn
Favorite Books: i don't read

Contact Information —————————————————————————

AIM Screen Name: monkeyboner82

Bob Ross, peerless PBS painter rounds out the list of Bobs. Who but he could captivate hordes of probably stoned Trustafarians for hours without music or vivid animation? His gentle voice constantly reminds Trustafarians that "there are no mistakes . . . only happy accidents," and they are transfixed, no longer upset about the happy accidents in life. In each episode and in just a half-hour, Ross turns a blank canvas into what Trustafarians imagine outside to be like. They are wowed.

Ross died many years ago, but you would never know, as this Julia Child of landscapes keeps painting on public television.

JUDAISM AND REGGAE

If you have ever been to a Seder (the family ritual meal of Pesach, or Passover), there is a good chance that any singing around the table did not follow a reggae beat. However, there are strong connections between Judaism and the Rastafari movement. The emblematic Rastafari lion is in fact the Lion of Judah. It is not, therefore, so strange that Jewish people find a gateway into the music of the Rastafari. This increasingly common culture mix is the perfect niche interest for Trustafarians.

The most notable figure in this blend is Matisyahu. To hear this Hasidic reggae star sing, one would think he has the dark skin of many reggae artists, but he is as pale as Nicole Kidman.

With TV appearances, a number 28 spot on the *Billboard Hot 100*, and his traditional garb (while his backup band wears T-shirts), Matisyahu is the most well-known face of Jewish Reggae, but he is not alone. He is in the company of other artists like David Gould, Ron Wiseman, and King Django, who would probably gain more notice among Trustafarians if they took the last name of Marley.

The mix of Jewish and Rasta cultures extends beyond music. The 2001 film *Brooklyn Babylon* follows the rocky relationship of a Rastafarian and a Jewish girl. The 2005 documentary *Awake Zion* explores the similarities between the two cultures.

This road between the Rastafari movement and Judaism is certainly not one-way. Rastafarians can certainly look forward to a slew of new holidays to celebrate, but it may be difficult stuffing all those locks into a yarmulke.

FIGURE 8.b. *Come Hanukkah, the menorah will not be the only thing lit for eight nights.*

Social Networking Sample: **Heirasite**

Katie Potvin wants new friends lol

Info

Basic Information _____

Name: Katie Potvin
Religious Views: i'll convert, lol
Political Views: some, but not too many, enough to have an opinion, but not too much to be all political

Likes and Interests _____

Favorite Music: i like all kinds except country
Favorite Movies: Annie? i dunno lol
Favorite TV Shows: i don't watch a lot of tv. i like to go out and find friends.
Favorite Books: i don't read

Contact Information _____

AIM Screen Name: bonbonQT84

Trustafarians do not really like a lot of things. This chapter pretty much covers the extent of anything noteworthy. If you want to find out more about Trustafarians' tastes in entertainment, talk to people in their early thirties and ask them what they liked in high school, and then factor in the Internet (inclusive of pornography for both genders, and flash cartoons for men) for a well-rounded scope.

Turn Your Trustafarian into a Trustafarian Pop Culture Icon!

Becoming a renowned Trustafarian is not easy to do, as achieving fame requires a level of effort most Trustafarians cannot stomach. It is not impossible though, if you take on the burden on your Trustafarian's behalf. There is not much in it for you, but the cultural enigma you created will certainly be getting a shout-out in a revised edition of *The Trustafarian Handbook*.

Method 1: Set Up a Webcam.

This will be a live feed showcasing all of your Trustafarian's movements (or lack of them) at home. Believe it or not, there is a large misinformed portion of the population that despises members of the Trustafari. They simply do not understand that they have their own trials to face. They will come expecting to loathe what they see. They will leave with a bevy of mixed emotions, ranging from pity to joviality. They will return in an attempt to sort out these feelings, and they won't be able to turn away. A Trustafarian is just too perplexing. Their brooding stares and enchanting but bizarre antics will prevent them from ever being nexted on Chatroulette. Do not settle for one on one video chats though, your Trustafarian is bigger than that. Find a web hosting service with a dedicated server to handle your traffic.

FIGURE 8.c. *Nudity in 3 . . . 2 . . . 1 . . .*

Make sure you have a disclaimer that states that your Trustafarian's webcam cannot be viewed by minors, as within the first three live minutes, there will be boobs or a penis.

CONTINUED ON NEXT PAGE

Method 2: Succeed where Lance Bass Did Not.

Remember Bass, former pop singer, and current grounded astronaut? Apparently he needed about $20 million to make his space flight but could not come up with the adventure capital. Does your Trustafarian get that sort of coinage in a birthday card? Or could he/she ask for it during a surprise visit home? Could he/she just take it from the trust fund directly?

It is unlikely that your Trustafarian is terribly open about his/her finances, so Google his/her parents and figure out how much they have.

Once in space, the Trustafarian should perform one of the following tasks: convert the other astronauts to the Rastafari movement or give them dreadlocks, eat a pot brownie, tag the space station with a pot leaf, or moon the Earth. The eyes of the entire world will be on your Trustafarian. He/she will surely be an answer in the next edition of *Trivial Pursuit*.

FIGURE 8.d. *Stoned in Space.* *"ASS-tronaut . . . heh heh."*

A fun bonus for this method to fame is that you may be flown to NASA or the Russian Federal Space Agency to help your Trustafarian cheat his/her way through space camp.

Method 3: Reveal Plans for Trustopia.

All right, this one involves so much planning that friends of Trustafarians rarely say "Trustopia" aloud. Imagine if you will, a manmade island floating in the Pacific. Its inhabitants are Trustafarians from around the world, and of course you, who inspired it.

Trustopia is expensive. No one can afford it. However, a conglomeration of trust funds from around the globe can—and could probably even afford to make the island fly. Imagine zipping around the world on Trustopia!

CONTINUED ON NEXT PAGE

Trustafarians are the only social group who could make this work. They have the money. They are also usually unwanted by society, so governments will let them go only slightly less readily than prisoners.

To be an independent nation, a country must be recognized as independent by other countries. Easily done! Some of the poorer countries in the world will be paid off in exchange for this recognition. An independent nation must also have some sort of established population. Trustafarians do not want to return home. They will be permanent residents.

Explain this to your Trustafarian, focusing mostly on how he/she will get to be president of the floating island nation. Next get the other Trustafarians on board. Start with the networking Brohemians. Tell the Fauxlanthropists that your country will need artists. Tell them all that life's stress will be nations away and that marijuana will be legal. If you can get the ball rolling, Trustafarians will sustain monetary momentum. You will need to be the focused project director throughout Trustopia's formation, often working in the shadows.

Your President Trustafarian will become legend, thanks to you! Your efforts will be forgotten, but at least you will know the truth and have a sweet flying nation to call your home.

Seeing That Buttoned-Up
WASP Lady Lose Her Shit

Trustafarians may spend 99 percent of their time in the various apartments they rent, but home is where the money is. As little as they want to be there and as little as anyone really wants them there, visits are necessary. Unconditional love binds Trustafarian families together like any other, despite any rampant dysfunction.

Visits home are often weekly, for those Trustafarians living within an hour radius of home, except when they have excuses or the parents are at their summer homes or vacationing—or when there is rain, wind, a solstice, new episodes of *Top Chef,* or a promising nap. For those outside the hour barrier, visits are often tri-annual but last for a week or more.

What Trustafarians Expect from Their Homecoming

Upon first entering a former home the Trustafarians are reminded of their past. They see the piano no one ever learned how to play, even though at one point they promised they would. They may notice that ugly thing they painted in ninth grade has been taken down and replaced by some sort of decorative plate. At least one of the rooms has probably been redecorated since the last visit because Mom has a lot more free time since she has stopped worrying about her kid. The Trustafarian is generally happy with the changes, as the old décor had many bad memories associated with it.

Photos of the Trustafarians in their younger days may be displayed prominently, showing a happy young boy in a button-down shirt with adorable glasses and a wide, braced smile or a young girl with a becoming side ponytail and jumper. These remind Mom and Dad of what might have been.

FIGURE 9.a. *Trevor Ryan Farrell: before and after*

Another common find in the old home is an assortment of pill bottles, all prescribed by doctors who are notable family friends. The bar has probably never been better stocked. That will change quickly.

There will also likely be a family portrait of Dad and Mom (or his new wife and family), but the Trustafarian will probably be absent—a sigh of relief on everyone's part. They tend to steal focus in photographs.

A Trustafarian is not likely to recognize his/her childhood room. If he/she does, then you should question the things that made you assume he/she was a Trustafarian to begin with. It takes a certain amount of pushing the baby out of the nest to create a Trustafarian, and, of course, a certain amount of love, a vestige of the original motherly instinct that made her keep the kid in the first place. By making the nest inhospitable, a mother ensures her child will not come crawling back—so much as she can help it.

If the Trustafarian is staying overnight, accommodations will likely be made in the puppy habitat room or behind the bar with a sleeping bag. They will not get the guest room though, as the guest room is reserved for guests. Since Trustafarians' money comes from the family home, the Trustafarians are anything but guests.

A Trustafarian may also not recognize the people who live in the old home. It is not uncommon for POTs to move on a whim and forget to tell everyone. If that happens, it is behooving for a Trustafarian to save the key, as the home may prove useful as a hiding place or vacation home when the new owners are away. Immediately though, the Trustafarian will have to call his/her parent and find out where the new home is and let them know that he/she will be late. Oftentimes, parents will move only blocks away, just for a change of pace in their carefully chosen neighborhoods.

A New Home for the Heirasite

It will be hinted strongly by parents that Trustafarians' friends are not invited to family night/weekend. This will not stop the Heirasite friends, who are siphoning every possible morsel of the life they were not given. The legitimate Trustafarians either do not register the heavy hinting or just look forward to the disappointment on their parents' faces when an expected but unwanted plus-one shows up at the door.

Heirasites help provide their primary Trustafarians with company during the uncomfortable visits. They, unlike the primaries, do qualify for guest rooms and are generally told to sleep there after they are found passed out in the bathroom, in the dining room, or on an occupied sofa. They may also opt to share the puppy habitat room or behind-the-bar space with their primaries.

A Heirasite may seem docile, but will likely try to sleep with a family member (not their own) during their stay—anything that makes them an irremovable part of the family. It is instinctive and generally effective.

Family Fun

Activities are dependent on individual family preferences, which are often determined by wealth and geography.

FOOTBALL

A very common family activity is football. Dad bought himself a new pair of athletic shoes because a cute blond at Sports Chalet talked him into it, and now he wants to use them. The old cow-skin gets dusted off and the men of the family and any particularly spunky females are divided up into teams.

Would a Trustafarian enjoy this? No. Never. Parents are smart though, and know that they are the hosts for their parasitic brood. Cars and apartments can easily be taken away for refusing to participate in family fun. Football quickly

FIGURE 9.b. *The greatest innovation to balls since the sphere*

becomes a façade for the Trustafarian's real game: breaking up the merriment and quickly ending the game, at any cost. Touch football may quickly become violent tackle football. This is an especially easy switch for the female Trustafarians, who can just attribute savage violence to their spunkiness. Other quick game-enders include throwing the football into the top branches of a tree or inducing dad's heart attack.

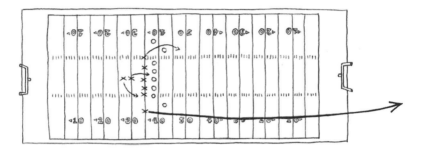

FIGURE 9.c. *Going as long as possible. The bold arrow represents the Trustafarian's victory/exit strategy.*

BADMINTON

Here is a sporting option for those less rugged families. Badminton is actually fairly easy and fun. You can easily smoke or drink with one free hand while the rest of your body is involved in the game. The only potential pitfalls for Trustafarians are getting the shuttlecock (easily the most enjoyable ball name in sports) stuck in their hair and accidentally revealing that a good time is being had.

POKER

Poker is another option but generally a mistake, as regardless of the outcome, Dad is losing money. At some point he will become aware of this and yelling will begin. Being involved in a poker chip fight may seem fun at first, but someone will usually be smacked with an octagonal table, ending the politely masked disdain.

FIGURE 9.d. *An American C-list celebrity obsession from 2003 to 2006*

SOLITUDE

A popular togetherness substitute is time spent apart. While Dad, Mom, or whoever has been hired to cook preps the evening supper, Trustafarians and other family members can retire to separate spaces on the large properties or in the large city apartments. This is one rare instance where Trustafarians might bring a book with the intent of reading it. A Trustafarian can never be sure if parents have shipped off his/her former possessions to a storage facility, so bringing along something to pass the time is generally a good idea.

Solitude does not have to involve literally being alone. Many families choose to mix cocktails, sit down, and not talk for a solid hour. Every so often, someone will sigh to help the tension.

Meals

Family meals force families to be together. Without them, children might not eat their veggies and parents might get to know Vanna and Pat more than their children. For all the family tables missed while their Trustafarians were young, parents force their families together more than ever in their children's adulthood. It is an attempt to make reparations.

THE PRIX FIXE MENU

A lot of effort will go into meal preparation so as to stave off the yelling-match portion of the evening as long as possible. Trustafarians can be tremendously picky eaters due to their whimsical diets. Here is an example of a well-planned family meal with alternate considerations for Trustafarians as well.

Course the First
Gorgonzola Puffed Pastries,
paired with Bordeaux
Or
Bordeaux

꽃

Course the Second
Seared Ahi Tuna Salad,
tastefully arranged like a water lily,
paired with cold sake
Or
Sake, and a salad to look at

꽃

Course the Third
Alaskan King Crab Cake,
topped with red pepper aioli, paired
with Chilean sauvignon blanc
Or
Velveeta Shells & Cheese

꽃

Course the Fourth
Whole-Wheat Pasta in a
Mango Cream Sauce, paired with
Dad's homemade pinot noir
(really a generic red)
Or
Artisan Cheese Plate

꽃

Course the Final
Artisan Cheese Plate (what is left),
paired with both red and white ports
in copious amounts
Or
An Excuse to Leave the Table,
paired with a middle finger and
no one impressed

꽃

Why the Yelling Starts

No one is surprised when it happens, as it always does. It is no one's fault more than any one else's—except parents. Trustafarians are not ticking time bombs of anger shrapnel. They are more like cartoon bombs, and it is the parents who light the fuse.

The parents are often blind to their own attacks, which come from a place of great jealousy. One or both of them has worked their whole lives to provide a nurturing environment for Trustafarians, and it is obvious that they have been successful. They have children who are successful and financially well off without having to do anything. Parents look at their children and regret that their own parents did not do the same for them, unless the Trustafarian's parents are also Trustafarians. In that rare situation, there are no weekly or tri-annual gatherings, and there is certainly much less yelling.

Trustafarians do hold a lot of guilt and shame all on their own. They regret being given so much, but they are also tired of everyone wanting them to feel bad for it. They also cannot be expected to reject what they have been given—at least not literally.

They reject what they have been given *symbolically*. They turn their backs on most things that remind them of the rich world that birthed them. They find luxuries that can fit nicely within their adopted squalor. They are able to internalize all of their guilt and shame, living their seemingly guiltless and shameless lives—just like the poor. They have had at least eighteen years of practice at this internalization, so outwardly they are complacent and perfect. The result is children who have everything but do not resemble their families that provided it.

Because of that Mom and Dad are seething.

Mom and Dad are also proud. They created these effortless successes through their own hard work, but showing that pride can be dangerous. Trustafarians, having rejected the rich, generally white way of living, would see pride and run even farther away. Disappointment keeps them visiting.

Parents also want their dues. They want thanks but they also want to put their children through a coal walk so the thanks are packed with remorse, shame, and honesty.

It is always a complicated and tumultuous mix of emotions when commingling the successful parents and their greatest successes: the Trustafarians.

WHAT WILL CAUSE THAT WASP LADY TO LOSE HER SHIT

1. Realizing her child is too gross or unrecognizable to hug
2. Being macked on by a Heirasite
3. Being Marsha Bradied with football (guaranteed game ender)
4. Seeing husband cry first
5. Being called a "cracker" at the table
6. Finding out Nana ate one of the special brownies
7. Seeing husband get macked on by Heirasite in her bed

TRUSTAFARIAN SPOTLIGHT ON

Erik and Lyle Menendez

Brothers Erik and Lyle grew up in a time when the term *Trustafarian* did not even exist. Had it been around for them to shape their identities, they may have made some different choices (or come up with a better secret-keeping strategy).

If you do not remember these brothers, shame on you. Father Jose was a millionaire and mom spent her days worrying about her children. Worrying did not help. Erik and Lyle said goodbye to her and her husband with a shotgun, and then went to see *Batman* (the Michael Keaton/Jack Nicholson one).

In the months following the unsolved murder, the brothers went on extravagant shopping sprees.

Erik and Lyle Menendez

—continued

One of them made a boob by telling his therapist about his shotgun bastardization, and the therapist gabbed—and it had been such a good plan!

Erik and Lyle steal the spotlight for two reasons: 1) Trustafarians can pull the "at least I'm not a Menendez brother" excuse anytime a parent is upset, and 2) They prove that even Trustafarians can make something of themselves: Orphans.

Siblings: Trustbrothers and Trustsisters

With many resources and a lot of money, many Trustafarians' parents only opt to bring one child into the world. It allows their benefits to be entirely funneled into one person instead of dividing them among multiple children, decreasing per capita value. They can also afford to keep their child safe and healthy with the highest-quality education, medical care, and security detail. They do not need a second child as a contingency plan.

Circumstances may arise where multiple children are birthed. Some mothers may be particularly religious, while others may be historically irregular and end up on one of those TLC specials for women who did not realize they were pregnant. Other times, parents may not be pleased with their first child so they try again (and again). Whatever the cause, a Trustafarian may have siblings with which to cope and possibly contend.

ARISTOBRATS

These are the younger, sexier versions of their parents. The parents find this offensive because it is insulting to show that they can be improved upon. Aristobrats are also thorns in the sides of the Trustafarian siblings, who view them as noisy and difficult to look at. They are the nightmare versions of the

Trustafarians' selves, often combining unnaturally white teeth and unnaturally shiny hair.

Not all Aristobrats wear pastels, khakis, and play tennis, which is the stereotype most people have in mind. Some are supremely metrosexual. Some are celebrities. Some are suburban.

When the football and badminton begins, the Aristobrats will generally reveal themselves by quickly calling the position of team captain and then suggesting their nemeses, the Trustafarians be the other team captain. The Aristobrat captain always picks the highest-ranking family member to be on his/her team. This ensures a shared victory drink and further bonding. To Trustafarians, this is simply gross. They can easily find themselves saddled with a dementia-suffering aunt and a fat little cousin, while facing off against an Aristobrat brother, father, and uncle, who were all college football stars.

The Trustafarians are not jealous. They could care less if they are the favorite. They are annoyed because it is difficult to listen to hours of chatter about BOTOX, portfolio management, class reunions, and sizeable donations.

Sometimes, POTs may strongly urge that Aristobrats take their Trustafarian siblings out with them socially, either to shop for some nice clothes or to meet some new people on a more respectable evening out. A true Aristobrat will smile and say how that sounds like a great idea but then shortly after, pull the Trustafarian aside and demand that he/she find an excuse not to go or suffer vague consequences.

A chess match between two very bored siblings: Jeremy and Francis Spaulding-Mars. Jeremy is twenty-seven and earns money from bootlegging Netflix DVDs and being Julianne Spaulding's son. Francis is twenty-five, the director of sales at a B2B marketing firm, Julianne Spaulding's son, and a lifetime member of Crunch Gym. He is also engaged, an SAT prep tutor, a guest sports columnist for the *San Francisco Chronicle*, a former Youth Entrepreneur of the Year, and a volunteer firefighter, who once saved two people from choking in a single day. Here is how their game went.

TURN	MOVE	COMMENT
Francis	King's pawn to e4	"I always kicked your ass at chess."
Jeremy	King's pawn to e5	No comment
Francis	Knight to f3	"I might be the company's youngest VP."
Jeremy	Knight to c6	"Remember when your prom date said you raped her?"
Francis	Bishop to b5	"Remember when you didn't accomplish anything?"
Jeremy	Rook to e3	No comment.
Francis	No move	"Asshole, that's not a real move."
Jeremy	Francis' Queen to Francis' forehead	"Neither is this."
Francis	Knight, Bishop, Rook, etc. to floor	"Pick those up!"
Jeremy	Smirk	"Let's get your slut fiancé in here, and have her do it."
Francis	Hands to Jeremy's throat	"Grow up, Jeremy!"
Jeremy	Knee to Francis' groin, loogie to Francis' mouth	"Take it, you corporate bitch!"
Mom	Alcohol to gullet	"You guys want to take a ride to look at the autumn leaves?"
Jeremy	Hands to sides	"I just guess . . . I'm jealous of you."
Francis	Hesitation	No comment.
Jeremy	Francis through glass coffee table, Jeremy out door.	"Checkmate!"

Outwardly, the parental motivation for this odd-couple pairing is to lift a Trustafarian out of his/her squalor and show the multitude of options available if their child is willing to work for it.

On a subconscious level, the parents are punishing their Aristobrat for daring to upstage them. Certainly their Trustafarian is a little bit gross, but that is not threatening. They created this leech, and while they may not agree with the outward manifestations of his/her freedom, they certainly accept that the Trustafarian is enjoying life in a special Trustafarian way.

A lot of people wonder why Aristobrats are not a Trustafarian type. It is because they made one major mistake. They built their own safety net. If all stipends were cut off to all trust fund children, Aristobrats could keep on going. Little to no changes would occur in their lifestyle. They have a job that pays as much if not more than they need to be comfortable. They could kiss their families goodbye and never look back.

In the same situation, Trustafarians would panic. They would wonder how they are possibly expected to live as the people they camouflage themselves among. Apartments might be lost. Alarm clocks would need to be purchased, because poor people have those. Poor people also have jobs that they are not really free to leave whenever they like—a peculiar concept for the Trustafarian and one that would not quite sink in until a few firings down the road. It would be the end of Trustafarian life as they know it.

MORE TRUSTAFARIANS

If it can happen once, it can happen again. Trustafarians can come in twos, threes, and mores. Trustafarians of the same type will get along. Many parents try to force their children into friendship. Never has this been so easy. Impostafarians can share their religious beliefs. Fauxlanthropists can find a creative way to hit up Mom and Dad for money to host some sort of fundraising circus. Brohemians can share stories of their inebriated high jinks, and Diddlysquatters can take naps or grunt in each other's company.

In pairs or groups they provide solace and escape from the rest of the family. In football it is much easier to intentionally fail and make it look like an earnest effort if two people work together. Bad throws and worse attempts to receive easily run up the other team's score to the agreed upon, game-ending total. Badminton becomes a team effort to hit the Aristo-brat in the face with a shuttlecock. With poker, other family members just become an audience to the real game, which is a contest of obscene bets and raises. It escalates quickly, and for Trustafarians really ads a bit of enjoyment to a generally uninteresting table game.

Whether weed, Red Stripe, gin, or some other substance is their coping mechanism of choice, Trustafarians can always slip off together to enjoy it. In these moments they will often consider sharing their goods because their Trustbrother or Trustsister is family, and they only have one of those, which they have for life.

Cross-type Trustafarian pairing does not go so smoothly.

Pairing: Impostafarian and Fauxlanthropist
COMPATIBILITY: Not too bad . . . at first
They can both get high and brainstorm about ways to heal Earth, right up until the Impostafarian realizes his/her sibling is white, and then things go downhill fast.

Pairing: Impostafarian and Brohemian
COMPATIBILITY: There's gonna be a fight
The Impostafarian is upset the Brohemian is not doing anything with his time on Earth and wants him to join the Impostafari. The Brohemian points out repeatedly that the Impostafarian is not black, until tiring of arguing and opting for fists.

Pairing: **Impostafarian and Diddlysquatter**

COMPATIBILITY: Frustratingly dull

The Impostafarian can pontificate all he/she wants. The Diddlysquatter will not listen and will also not react. The Impostafarian eventually tires.

Pairing: **Fauxlanthropist and Brohemian/Diddlysquatter**

COMPATIBILITY: Fleeting

There really is not anything to talk about. Dislike of Mom and Dad can only go so far. If Fauxlanthropists are lucky, their siblings may play an instrument and they can collaborate on some sort of ineffectual protest song.

Pairing: **Brohemian and Diddlysquatter**

COMPATIBILITY: Meh/Decent

Drinking and smoking will often pique Brohemians' interest in the fascinating lives of people other than themselves. "What's it like being _____?" is a common structure. If left with a Diddlysquatter, the Brohemian will at some point lean forward and ask, "How do you exist?" His/her curiosity is real, just wanting to understand the weird world a little bit better. The Diddlysquatter is pleased so long as no one is yelling or asking him/her to do things.

FAMILY SECRETS

Sometimes Trustafarians luck out and there exists a sibling even more offensive than they are. A Family Secret is a special type of child. Perhaps it is a killer, fresh out of prison. It may be a particularly flashy transsexual. A Family Secret may have a developmental challenge that is not cute or cause-friendly, or it just may

FIGURE 9.e. *Family Secret storage. You do not want to know.*

be part of Dad's Vietnam family. Whatever the reason, Trustafarians find they are no longer at the bottom of the barrel and may even receive open praise and compliments from parents, usually with a few insults as subtext.

Sloth from *The Goonies* is an excellent example of a Family Secret's potential.

Grandparents

And Trustafarians thought Mom and Dad were bad! While they have a lot in common with old folks, Trustafarians often find themselves at odds with the ones in their own families. Grandparents do not ride on their own pride as their children do. They consider the family a single unit, only as strong as its weakest member. If they are of sound enough mind to realize a Trustafarian is not working hard to be successful, they will say something, using those sharp and slightly racist, OPC insults only an old person can provide. Trustafarians will spend their entire trip avoiding the grandparents. Football, or anything that involves running, is useful as an escape.

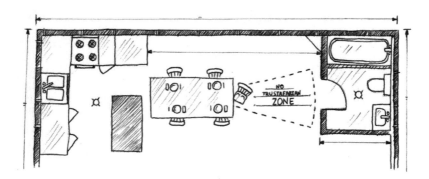

FIGURE 9.f. *No Trustafarian Zone. There exists a channel between the bathroom and the nearby hard-backed chair where a grandparent will settle. Chances of encountering a grandparent in this zone are 100 to 500 percent higher than anywhere else in the house. Trustafarians will do well to avoid this area.*

WHAT GRANDMA REALLY MEANS

Grandparent: Are you still tutoring?
MEANING: *Where's your real job?*

Grandparent: Where did you two meet?
MEANING: *You're not using that Internet—are you?*

Grandparent: How's your friend?
MEANING: *Are you still dating that black boy?*

Grandparent: You're not still a vegetarian—are you?
MEANING: *You're a fatty and a disappointment.*

Grandparent: Kimberly (or other name) is getting married.
MEANING: *No one wants you here!*

There are a few circumstances that will mitigate grandparent-Trustafarian tensions.

1. Grandparent was a hippie and Trustafarian brings back the good times.
2. Grandparent is not sure to whom he/she is talking.
3. Grandparent hates own child more than grandchild.

The third scenario is the most beneficial to Trustafarians, who will feel loved but only as a tool to hurt their parents. Their hair may even receive compliments for being fun or unique.

Here's what to do if you encounter your Trustafarian's grandparent:

Stay Calm

The worst thing you can do is panic. Grandparents will sense that you are trying to join their family. They do not want you. They have handpicked their genes. They also have great power and can easily have you removed from the premises in a way that parents are too polite to attempt.

Act Like You Are Valuable

If you are a bank security guard or work the register at any store, say that you work in finance. You are being vetted, so hype yourself. Nothing is too impressive, so, as long as you will not be caught in the lie, try it.

Rat Out Your Trustafarian

This is the only way to prove you are a friend more than someone who is after your friend's benefits. Tell Grandma something awful that your Trustafarian did and that you are very concerned. You want to be sure that your Trustafarian stays safe and makes good decisions. Let her know you will be her inside guy and take care of her grandchild.

Check the Legitimacy of the Grandparent

Does he/she look like the rest of the family? There is always a possibility that the grandparent is actually a Scamparent. Sometimes sweet old friends of the family will be adopted and treated like grandparents just because they do not have a family of their own or because their circumstances seem particularly sad. The Scamparent's motivation is very old but not kind. They want financial security and one of those fancy retirement villages where they throw parties after six and still have sex. You are a threat to their financial and future security. Money that goes to you will not go to them. The good news is that your secrets will be safe with one another. The bad news is that they are out to get you, so be careful.

Last Resorts

Scamparent or not, if you are in a tight spot with one of these old folks, you need to get out. You can try and stall and hope they need to pee or take a nap. If that does not work, you will need to attempt these last-ditch efforts. If you are in open space, run. If you are in a closed space, try having sex with the grandparent. Other than that, you are pretty much out of nonviolent options. Prepare for verbal abuse and threats to be carried out if you ever dare to return to the property again. All of your hard work is defeated, but only for the moment. You have generations to outlive the grandparent, so bide your time and make your move, perhaps with a heartfelt speech at a funeral.

Introducing the Girlfriends, Boyfriends, and Sexy Bedmates

MOM: It's not that we care if Donald has sex in the house. We just want to be sure that when we write you those child support checks that we did everything we could to prevent it.

Parents want the best for their children, but even the richest moms and dads have to be somewhat realistic. If their kid is a Trustafarian, there are going to be some insurmountable limits on the quality of mates he/she can reel in.

Whenever possible, Trustafarians keep their personal lives separate from their families, as most of the time, only unpleasantness can come from mixing the two. There are, however, a few occasions where a Trustafarian will bring someone home to meet Mom and Dad.

The first is, if by either browsing informative Facebook photos or hiring a private investigator, a mom finds out her Trustafarian is in a relationship that seems either long term or questionable—or maybe the companion seems particularly appealing—she may insist on a meeting.

Parents may also just really want to meet a daughter-in-common-law or son-in-common-law out of curiosity because their child's relationship is exceptionally long term or because they want to know if they need to exclude anyone from the will.

Believe it or not, there are reasons a Trustafarian would want to bring a significant or insignificant other home to meet the parents. The Trustafarian may be coupled with someone particularly unsavory, which would provide hours of entertainment at parents' expense. The weekend at home just might be bearable.

Also, if a Trustafarian is shacking up with someone who is not particularly trustworthy, the Trustafarian may insist the bedmate come along on a family visit, rather than be left alone in the apartment. Oftentimes though, ending the relationship and changing locks is a more appealing option.

However it comes about, once or twice in every sexually active Trustafarian's life, the person with whom he/she is sleeping will have to hang out with Mom and Dad. Parents are not expecting greatness. Parents only hope that their Trustafarian child will do what they do best—latch on to someone else and exploit the situation.

DAD: Have you come here to ask me something about my daughter?
MIKE "BAKED LAYS" O'NEILL: Yeah. You'll pay for the wedding—right?

There is usually disappointment for parents, often owed to Trustafarians acting out of spite. Their child's dates will be met with genuine curiosity, which soon dissipates into coldness.

Advice for the Trustafarian's Date

If you happen to be a Trustafarian's nubile plaything, no one will envy you. You are probably unaware that upon arriving at the Trustafarian's home, generally three different sleeping accommodations are made for you. One is with the Trustafarian, in the rare circumstance that the parents decide they like you. One is not with the Trustafarian, but in a cozy guest room with Internet, On Demand, and some sort of orthopedic mattress. This is the room you will get if you are shrugged at and accepted. The Trustafarian could do worse.

Then there is the most popular accommodation of all. Often cramped, and sometimes even vertical, this sleeping situation, whatever form it takes, is often difficult to imagine existing in such a nice home, but it is there. It is waiting for every little bitch or jackass (choice parental terms) that is ruining their child in a way parents could not.

During your stay, prepare to have each of your life choices examined. Prepare to talk about your parents, because POTs would love to have another rich couple with whom to commiserate. They do not like you and your parents will not like their Trustafarian. It is an opportunity for POTs to make new friends.

Prepare to watch some old white folks think they can slip irony into every sentence as an undertone that you could not possibly understand. Everything about you will be "different," "interesting," or like "something [they] saw in one of those magazines." It will be "refreshing to have someone like you in the neighborhood," and their son or daughter is "so lucky to have you."

Do your best to make these people like you. You have clearly chosen to be with a Trustafarian for a reason. Whether it is financial security, the thrill of your partner's unique lifestyle, love, or the fact that you happen to be extremely unattractive, try to keep in mind that the visit will not last forever. You will outlive the parents. It is only a matter of time.

TRUST FUN! | # Discover Your Trustafarian's Rich Person Nickname!

From Emily "Pemmy" du Pont Frick and Kathleen "Kick" Kennedy to Her Royal Highness, Queen Elizabeth "Lilibet" II of the United Kingdom, rich people have three things in common: wealth, power, and wackadoo nicknames. What's your Trustafarian's? Here is how you find out.

OPTION 1: Use the trip to the parents' place to your advantage. The Trustafarian will never admit having a rich person nickname, but you might get lucky and hear Mom call it out upon seeing her little one return.

OPTION 2: If the parents do not readily reveal the rich person nickname, just ask. This gives them a welcomed chance to embarrass their offspring while reliving the simpler days of decades ago.

OPTION 3: If your Trustafarian managed to steer the conversation away from his rich person nickname, wait until the part of the evening where everyone gets drunk. This part of the evening always happens. Ask again then. Try playing the name game and ask for funny suggestions if you have to. It might seem like a lot of work, but learning the rich person nickname is something you can mercilessly hold over your Trustafarian. If your Trustafarian ever mistreats you, you can threaten to reveal it.

OPTION 4: Get yourself drunk and say your Trustafarian's first name over and over again until weird things come out of your mouth (words, not vomit). You should eventually reach a point in your yammering where the Trustafarian seems offended. This means that you have just bastardized his name into his rich person nickname. Well done!

Most rich person nicknames are generally formed when a rich youth has a delightful speech impediment and cannot say a particular name properly. As a child grows and becomes less precious, the name is kept as a reminder of what once was.

Alcohol(ism)

(Belief in) alcohol is often the glue for Trustafarian families. Hardcore Impostafarians may disavow their drink, but their families will certainly enjoy it. Drinking starts in the morning, as anyone who enjoys an early brunch knows. It builds steadily through the rest of the day, being applied like a bandage with each new emotional cut wrought by conflict among Trustafarians, siblings, parents, grandparents, and peripheral wannabes. Near the end of the evening, there is a moment where everything becomes still. Everyone has been drinking, and for a moment, things are pleasant. Grandpa is passed out in the chair. A younger, innocent sister all of the sudden finds a dirty word in Boggle and everyone forgets themselves and laughs, tearing. Syrupy saxophone music starts to play either just in people's minds or by that stressed-out Asian kid who moved in next door. Mom may start flexing her weak arms in preparation for a hug. Dad might start to clear his throat for that apology speech he has been planning on making for the last fifteen years. Mom's new husband might be smiling, looking from face to face in the room, ready to forgive everyone else for making him and his wife miserable.

Then it is gone. What alcohol raises, it razes. Sis tries another off-color word and she is warned not to start acting like her Trustafarian sibling, who then begins yelling and maybe even throwing things. The WASP lady loses her shit, and things go to hell quickly. Doors slam, and one night of the happy trip is over.

Many fans of marijuana make the argument that weed tears apart far less families than alcohol, but how many does it bring together? Weed cannot unite people if people are unwilling to use it. Trustafarians' families do use alcohol, and more than anything else, it brings the families together—right before violently rending them.

BRAND NAMES LABEL THE POORER DRINKERS

Here is a tip to help you get a sense of the assets of a Trustafarian's family. This does not necessarily gauge whether a family is "Over six figures" or just "Well, you tried." It will however tell you just how classy they are as an effect of their wealth.

When you are offered a drink, is it a "rum and Coke" or a "Captain and Coke?" Adding a brand name to the alcoholic drink is an invention of an advertiser, not a consumer. ("Coke" doesn't count because the advertiser successfully obliterated the generic term from use.) If you are offered a brand-name liquor beverage, keep in mind that you are being offered status by a person who clearly misjudges his/her own. The super wealthy may drink the established name brands, but they do not flaunt it. Your gin is just gin and you trust its quality without any exotic, capital-lettered moniker to accompany it.

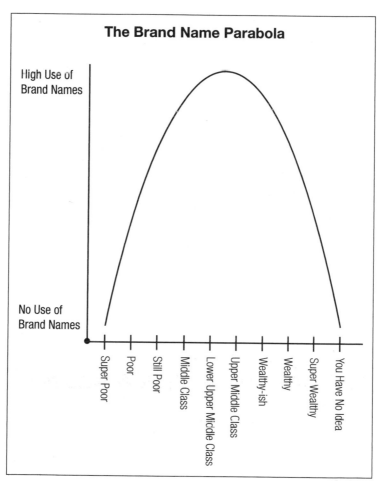

FIGURE 9.g. *If you take six or more things away from this handbook, make this one of them.*

CHAPTER 10

Trustafarian Calendar
For Those Who Can
Figure Out What Day It Is

Dear Parents of Trustafarians,

    Trustafarians do not forget your birthday because they do not love you. They forget it because forgetting things is part of their culture.

Holidays are very common and well-spread-out determinants of when to spend time together as a family. Here is a handy mini-guide to the major ones in Trustafarian life. (Sorry, Diwali fans.)

New Year's Eve
(begins on January 1 around 2:00 A.M.)

This is the big friend celebration of the year, though it may possibly include a date. There is no expectation for anyone to spend it with his/her family. Trustafarians will go out to celebrate, claiming it is just a normal night out. They will then proceed to be angered by all the New Year's celebrants clogging hallways and bars. As a result, most of the night will be spent in their apartments with a small, intimate group, making fun of televised events and performers.

Valentine's Day
(February 14)

Ditto.

St. Patrick's Day
(weekends surrounding and night of March 17)
Ditto.

Easter
(whenever Christ gets around to it)
Trustafarians and their families stopped celebrating Easter a decade after they stopped going to church, which was two decades ago. Jewish Trustafarian family members will celebrate (or ignore) "Passover/Pesach," and use words like "Plague-bearing spirit" and "temple."

TRUSTAFARIAN SPOTLIGHT ON

Jesus of Nazareth

Clearly the Christian case against him being a Trustafarian is supported by the idea that he sacrificed himself for the good of all people. That is excellent, but there are some other facts to look at. Most glaringly, he is the son of a deity, and he was living and dressing like a poor carpenter. In addition, he spent a ton of time with his bros, and he went off the grid for almost twenty years. His job was going around and telling stories to people and doing the occasional magic trick. Barring that savior bit, he was a Trustafarian, and perhaps even a Brohemian archetype.

Tax Panic
(April 17–19)
Once a year, a frantic phone call goes to Mom, Dad, or their accountant to see if a Trustafarian's taxes were done (whatever that might mean). A particularly comical parent will traditionally respond with "We agreed you would take care of them this year," and their child will hate them for it.

4/20

(April 20)

Today, the daily herb is honored. Trustafarians everywhere rejoice by smoking up, eating pot brownies, and drawing marijuana leaves on their arms with Sharpies. Just being in the presence of a Trustafarian (or any weed smoker) on this day will make you feel good about yourself and the world.

Earth Day

(April 22)

Fauxlanthropists will call their families and ask them what they are doing to go green and save the planet. No answer will be satisfactory, but it is nice for Mom and Dad to hear from their kid.

Mother's Day

(second Sunday in May)

Mom can have whatever she wants for dinner today. Her Trustafarian will not be there to complain. The flowers that the Trustafarian sent will likely be there, but probably not until the following Tuesday.

Memorial Day

(last Monday in May)

It is just too close to Mother's Day to warrant its own celebration. A Trustafarian may be invited to a family barbeque, but no one expects the Trustafarian to show up.

Bonnaroo Music Festival

(sometime in June)

Trustafarians from east of the Mississippi and the Midwest stream by the thousands to Manchester, Tennessee, for this outdoor music fest. Each year, it draws bigger-named performers, but Trustafarians can always count on good jam bands, reggae, and standup comedy (which has its own tent). Phish has played there, so Trustafarians usually do not need too much convincing. Plus, they love their vacations.

Bonnaroo usually lasts for four days, three of which Trustafarians spend trying to set up a tent and then ultimately paying someone else to do it.

ADVICE FOR TRAVELERS

Do not schedule flights out of Tennessee that coincide with the close of the Bonnaroo festival. While communal showers were made available for festivalgoers, many opted for the raw, natural experience. Never has a plane cabin felt more like the inside of an old lady neighbor's apartment, when it is discovered that she has been dead for eight weeks.

Father's Day
(third Sunday in June)

Remember that thing Dad always wanted? Neither do the Trustafarians. The only way he is going to get it is if he wanted a phone call sometime in the late evening from his child to say "Happy Father's Day!" and ask for money.

Fourth of July
(July 4)

America's birthday brings a weekend-long barbeque full of mandatory family time, football, and illegal fireworks that someone bought to look cool (nope) when setting them off in the backyard with people pretending to watch. Having not seen their kids yet this year, parents can usually squeeze a visit out of them for this holiday.

Marcus Garvey's Birthday
(August 17)

Most Trustafarians are not to sure what Marcus Garvey did—only that it has something to do with making many Jamaicans, black people, and Bob Marley respect him a lot. That alone is enough reason to celebrate not so much a man, but a particularly dry holiday season in August.

Burning Man
(last Monday in August through Labor Day)

As Bonnaroo is able to suck in all of the eastern U.S. Trustafarians, Burning Man draws the more western ones. Of course, that is not exclusive. There is a Trustafarian exodus out of every major city to go there. If you do not know what Burning Man is and you ask someone who has gone, the first thing he/she will say is, "You can't possibly understand if you haven't been." Whenever someone says that, it is just because they are worried you will not be impressed when they tell you.

There is a lot that goes on at Burning Man. It is an art festival, an active collective of artists and helpers turning the desert into a surreal landscape of sculptures—and then burning it to the ground. Each year a giant, titular statue of a man is burned, an effigy which Trustafarians figure must be representative of something awesome.

Most Trustafarians do not pretend to understand art—especially in terms of temporary desert sculpture. They just like to walk around naked and burn things.

Labor Day

(first Monday in September)

If someone was absent during the Fourth of July celebration, this is the make-up date, unless of course the Trustafarian is at Burning Man, in which case, this year's family visit will wait until Thanksgiving.

Halloween

(October 31)

Everyone goes to separate parties and does not tell each other how it went. Mom and Dad have more fun dressing up than the Trustafarians, who opt for either elaborate, expensive, but underappreciated costumes or just their street clothes, for which they will receive many incorrect guesses about what they are supposed to be.

TRUST FUN! | ## Costly Costumes!

If you are hanging with a Trustafarian on All Hallows' Eve, do not miss an opportunity to celebrate in a way you could never afford on your own! Help your Trustafarian choose a costume. Most people assume a costume is a showy piece made out of fabric, but that definition is stilted. For Trustafarians, costumes can involve fabric, electrics, vehicles, and even actors! If your Trustafarian has a hankering to dress up as Snow White, suggest that she (or he) hire a bunch of little people to play dwarves. Snow White and her posse will be the surefire winner for best costume at any party.

Here are some tips for a safe and elaborate Trustafarian Halloween:

Make sure prop guns are not loaded.

Or better yet, just leave guns out of the costume. This is especially important for Impostafarians. One misfire in a predominantly black neighborhood

CONTINUED ON NEXT PAGE

---

destroys any chance of sneaking into the community. For other Trustafarians, the legal issues involved in covering up a shooting are just burdensome. Do not take the chance. You may have to take the fall for it if there is no clean exit for your Trustafarian.

Even if the grassy knoll set has been built and the '61 Lincoln Continental Convertible already refurbished, suggest a sling shot or water pistol be used instead. It may seem lame, but it really is a smart choice. If your Trustafarian balks at the substitute, try suggesting some sort of sci-fi weapon for which the destructive technology does not quite yet exist.

Hire a stage manager.
If actors or models are involved, do not let your Trustafarian saddle you with the task of keeping them together and moving them as a group. Hire an outsider who has experience with these things.

Do not hire AEA or SAG members as props.
If you hire union performers, you will be subjugating your Halloween happiness to people who think that their art is just as important as your costume, which on this special night, it is not. What's more, there are a ton of rules. You are not giving them career breaks or appropriate credit. You are paying them in money and fun.

Beware of expensive, cliché costumes.
Blockbuster movies, sultry and sluttish celebutants, and politicians (during election years) are costume magnets. Those with a lot of disposable income can come up with these ideas and afford to make them look good without much effort. Even though dressing up as the graduating class of Hogwarts seems like a good idea, if you follow through, you may find yourself faced with a twin when you are out on the town. There can only be one. The better-costumed group will be the only ones accepted at the party. Either

CONTINUED ON NEXT PAGE

be prepared to stake your reputation on the quality of your costume and the hotness of your Hermione or just avoid it and go as something quirkier, like the Ghostbusters, unless it is a year when the next film is coming out.

Beware of hired models getting too chummy with your Trustafarian.

If the guy playing Grumpy seems to be smiling too much and your Trustafarian keeps shouting, "I love this guy!" intervene immediately or risk being replaced. Your position as a Trustafarian's friend is a fragile one. Find Grumpy a hot girl, or make him eat the prop poisoned apple.

Do not let your Trustafarian dress up in protest of something he/she does not understand.

Use your judgment. If your Trustafarian's ignorance is going to negatively affect your evening, talk him/her out of it.

Do not let your Trustafarian pretend to be a policeman.

If you dress up like Superman, you should not try to fly. If you dress up as a policeman, you should not try to arrest people or take up vigilante crime fighting. The actual police will get very upset. Costumes can go to people's heads. Never mind the hysterical use of the dildo as a billy club. Protect everyone by making smart but elaborate costume decisions.

Protect yourself.

Trustafarians are survivors. If they take you to a "scary" part of town with no lights, seedy-looking businessmen, bloodstains, and video cameras and you are separated, leave them. Trying to find them will only make things worse for you. Get yourself out of there safely. Days may pass before a Trustafarian returns home, but it will happen.

Thanksgiving

(fourth Thursday in November)

It is the most fancy two-course meal in America. It touts more side dishes than anyone wants, but rarely involves soup, even though it would be delicious. Thanksgiving can unfold in a few different ways. Traditionally Mom will be kept busy in the kitchen and Dad will be kept busy by the football game on TV. Neither is a particularly wanted option for Trustafarians, who will try to find some means of escape.

Conversely, Dad may have been watching a lot of Paula Dean lately and either be deep-frying his bird or stuffing it with the other pieces of a turducken. Mom will probably either be napping or chatting with friends and relatives. Trustafarians can back the napping, which allows them to share an activity with their mom, in separate rooms, apart. Visiting is, as you now know, not enjoyed. A Trustafarian may offer to take a long trip to the store to pick up a missing ingredient, possibly after destroying/hiding an ingredient to ensure it went missing.

When it comes time for the meal, a family will often observe an awkward pause to see if anyone is going to force them to say grace. It is generally up to the most important family member to take a deep breath and say, "Well this all looks wonderful." He/she will then proceed to eat, and everyone else will follow.

Trustafarians may use the meal to complain and make an example of how society does not accommodate vegetarians. The fact that there are fourteen vegetables in front of them is generally not part of their concern.

For many parts of the United States, Thanksgiving takes place on a cold day where outdoor sports are just implausible for anyone but professionals. The downside to this is that a family is trapped indoors. Tensions run considerably higher. Someone is storming off before dessert.

What Are Trustafarians' Families Thankful For?

- That everybody, with some notable exceptions, could make it to the meal
- That the weather was decent
- That *Futurama* came back

- For the Food Network
- That their economic downturn will end sooner than the poor's
- That someone is sober enough to blow into the breathalyzer

Jesus' Birthday
(December 25)

If you ask a Trustafarian what he/she got for Christmas, your Trustafarian will answer with this construction: "It was a very nice Christmas. I got . . ." + one of their least expensive gifts + another inexpensive gift + "and some other stuff."

This is a well-crafted play to look normal. They are smart enough to acknowledge that they at least appreciate they got anything at all, as any legitimate Tiny Tim would. They then list their least impressive items to show that they are not too spoiled, and then, they combine all the rest of their prize into a dismissive but still honest etcetera.

Eventually you will realize the scope of the truth. You may be asked for your number so it can be put into a new phone. You may notice a new motorcycle or that the number of maids has doubled. You may find your Trustafarian cancels plans because a Mexican cruise has suddenly come up. Yet when you asked what the Trustafarian got for Christmas you were told, "It was a good Christmas. I got a sweater, some Mounds, and some other stuff."

Be aware that often Trustafarians not only get Christmas presents on December 25. They may also receive sizeable gifts on each of the twelve days of Christmas. Many may find more than chocolate in their Advent calendars.

On this holiday, family gatherings become worth their hassles. Trustafarians will be excited to see the new stuff they own. The gifts they pick out for others will be interesting if nothing else—probably things available within two blocks of their apartment or still wrapped in their Amazon.com boxes.

In consideration of Jewish Trustafarians, please substitute "Hanukkah" and "not visiting home" as applicable.

Other Birthdays

(as needed)

Their own birthdays will be spent away from families and may involve anything from exotic vacations to parties at bars rented out just for them and a few friends who follow through on their Evite RSVPs. Gifts and money holding cards will come in the mail from relatives all week.

Parents' birthdays will also be spent away from families. Small gifts will be mailed, and phone calls will be made—not to say, "Happy birthday!" but, "Did you get the crap I sent you?"

Siblings' birthdays are not celebrated enough for any Trustafarian to be able to report back on what happens during those events. If any are spent with the siblings, they are the teenage ones, and they are spent drinking or finding fake IDs for Trustbrothers and Trustsisters. In this way, Trustafarians prepare their younger (possibly older) siblings for the world.

All Trustafarians must establish a balance between spending a little bit of time with their families and spending no time with their families. Too much time necessitates family involvement in the day-to-day nonsense that they would just rather handle alone. Too little brings with it the dangers of losing family support (financial, not emotional). They run the risk of losing their money to their siblings or a particularly loved family pet. They saw the gruesome consequences of this with Leona Helmsley, who willed loads of money to her canine and stiffed two of her grandchildren. Old rich people love to have the last laugh. It gives them mild comfort as they leave everything behind.

Trustafarians have to work relatively diligently to stay in the favor of their wealthy parents so they are not the butt of a dying person's joyous wrath. This means showing up to family events and vacations. It means being there when Aristobrats are home to make sure the brats do not turn their parents against them.

Trustafarians may not often exhibit street smarts or book smarts, but they are very intelligent and able to manipulate and carry out long-term strategies for the purpose of maintaining their status quo.

One tactic is reporting and exaggerating stories about the trouble that their crazy friends have gotten into. Parents will be glad their children are talking to them and thrilled that they are not taking part in such vulgarities.

Trustafarians may wait to report any bad news until after a parent has received worse news about something else. They may take good news and divide it into many smaller pieces of good news, so that it seems like an ongoing success streak.

Despite all the time apart and all the displeasure that occurs during family gatherings, parents will be content enough with the way their child's life has reached a rather uncomplicated plateau. It could be far worse. They know their children are only nice to them because they have to be, but at least the Trustafarians are being true to who they are. Many have described Trustafarians' family dynamics as dysfunctional, but really their economic position affords them no other way to exist. Trustafarians work their families and their funding just like regular people work their jobs—with halfhearted interest but out of dire necessity.

Gift Ideas for the Faux Pariah Who Has Everything

So, you want to buy your Trustafarian's love, but you're flat out of ideas? Well, worry not. Here is a tried-and-true list to help all of you stunted Saint Nicks pick the perfect presents. (Note the plural.)

DO TRUSTAFARIANS NEED PRESENTS?

Of course they do! Everyone needs presents unless they have taken a vow of poverty, and those votaries certainly are not Trustafarians. Presents are just a nice way to say, "Thanks for being alive," and while they will not admit it, Trustafarians like to feel a momentary justification for existence every now and again. They also like new stuff!

MIX CD

This is the perfect gift for a struggling Heirasite to give. Trustafarians understand that their supposed friends are not as well-to-do as they are, and that is why they like them in the first place. A mix CD says, "I am poor, but I tried . . . for you."

Here is how you make a mix CD. First, find a blank CD or DVD. CDs are obviously cheaper, but use whatever you have at home. Next, grab a Sharpie—and pick a fun color, because your smudged handwriting is really going to make this present pop. Write, "_____'s Mix," draw some festive squiggles, write "from" or draw a little heart, and write your name. Finally, hand it to your Trustafarian.

He/she is never going to play it. No one likes when you pretend to be a personal DJ, so it really does not matter that you did not put any songs on it. What matters is that your Trustafarian thinks you spent hours picking out the perfect songs that create an aural mosaic of your relationship.

BONNAROO GIFT SET

This is the perfect gift to be given by those who can afford it. What is ultimately included in the set is up to your discretion, but here are some important staples.

- Plane tickets to and from Tennessee and VIP tickets to the festival (for Trustafarian and a few guests)
- Six-room disposable luxury tent with attached hot tub
- Per diem for booze, etc.
- Survival kit with sunscreen, beef jerky, flashlight, and gallons of water
- Five-day cooler
- Climate control sleeping bag and queen-sized air mattress
- Power generator or those pee-powered batteries from Singapore
- Folding lifeguard chairs (to see above the crowd)

FLIP MINOHD CAMCORDER

It shoots high-def video on something the size of a smart phone. Your Trustafarian is sure to be the next Mumblecore star with this high-tech pocket gizmo. Feel free to go all-out and get this one engraved with a special message.

For those Trustafarians with far-reaching documentary or film interests, a better choice may be the Sony HDW-790 HDCAM. This professional-grade toy costs only a few thousand more than a year at Yale with housing.

WHY SHOULD YOU GET THEM PRESENTS?

The simple fact is Trustafarians just do not have it in them to care for a lot of people. There is often too much unfortunate self-loathing surrounding them to let many positive emotions escape. Even the Fauxlanthropists, purporting to help others, only do it because it feeds their egos and lets them feel a little like heroes.

Presents are a beeline to the unselfish fraction of a Trustafarian's heart. It is POTs vs. Heirasite vs. other Trustafarian friends in a battle that will decide who wins a Trustafarian's favor.

May the best gift-giver win.

YOUR SIX-MONTH-OLD CAR

This is a cheap gift for POTs but not suggested for Heirasites, who have never owned a car less than twelve years old. Donating a car to an underprivileged family or a convent is a nice gesture, but then you rarely get to see your sweet ride again. POTs, keep it in the family, and enjoy your newer, better, more-expensive wheels that you will get as a gift from yourself.

ELECTRIC SKATEBOARD

For those Trustafarians cool enough to roll around town on a plank but not motivated enough to propel anything, this is the pinnacle of ultimate utilitarian gifts. They may cost a few hundred dollars, but the Trustafarian will love it. Most Heirasites find it to be worth the investment.

Gift Bonuses: You will love the looks on diners' faces when they see a relatively frozen, moribund Trustafarian float by the restaurant window. Also, the wheels can be tricked out, and Trustafarians do enjoy that.

> ### DOWNLOADABLE CONTENT
>
> Always check to see if there are any Trustafarian-applicable iPhone apps. There is a game out there, called *Rasta Monkey*, that will make any Impostafarian squeal with delight.

HAZILY PURPOSED PARAPHERNALIA

You may come to regret the illegality of purchasing weed as a gift for the Trustafarian in your life. As an alternative, consider these accessories.

Herbal Vaporizers

These gadgets are perfect—though in no way whatsoever specifically targeted or marketed—for Trustafarians, who perhaps enjoy the active chemical components of some herbs. Some are pocket-sized and some are shaped like volcanoes! Without burning and creating harmful smoke, these doodads vaporize organic matter, and that vapor fills a chamber or a big balloon, from which a Trustafarian may suck to his/her contentment.

Rolling Machines

Perhaps your Trustafarian is not as nimble as he/she needs to be to pull off the toker image. These handy and inexpensive manual machines look like something off of the *Double Dare* obstacle course, with symmetrical rollers offering Trustafarians a way to do what their fingers cannot—roll that perfect joint.

> Rolling papers also make a good last-minute gift or a stocking stuffer if you are not comfortable giving the gift that is to be rolled inside them.

Luxury Hookahs

Hookahs come in forms more elaborate than the richest parents or their most stoned children can even imagine. Whether sleek, gold-plated, travel-sized, aerodynamic, equipped with a ceramic burn plate, reminiscent of a sex toy, or all of the above, these add a bit of class to Trustafarians' lives, which of course is generally frowned upon, but when it comes to upmarket herbware, they will love it.

SHOULD YOU WRAP YOUR PRESENT?

If you are a friend, yes, wrap it. If you are a family member, do not wrap. Just stick it in the mail and wait a few days for a phone call.

THE TRUSTAFARIAN HANDBOOK

This makes a great gag gift for the Trustafarians who have a sense of humor or by whom you would like to be smacked. Also, any book with strong marijuana themes will be appreciated, though likely never read.

CELEBRITY GUEST STAR

With enough money offered, Angelina Jolie, Matisyahu, a Marley son, and Gallagher will all come to help your Trustafarian celebrate an otherwise forgettable occasion. Seth MacFarlane may even come and do voices! Give your Trustafarian some warning though so that he/she does not invite people who are under the illusion that their Trustafarian friend is so very poor.

PAPER TOWELS, TOILET PAPER, A PLUNGER, SPONGES, ETC.

These may seem like unimpressive gifts, but how else is a Trustafarian going to get these items? It certainly will not be on his/her own. Once a year, help your Trustafarian stock up.

CASH

The greatest gift of all is a stack of twenty-dollar bills. Trustafarians do not even care if there is a card or envelope. The winning point here is that unlike credit card charges, which end up on a bill seen by parents' persnickety financial managers, cash sales are virtually anonymous. Giving cash is giving freedom. Give Trustafarians as much freedom as you can.

FIGURE 10.a. *Damian Marley may have been at the birthday party, but Andrew Jackson was the most adored celebrity.*

CHAPTER 11

Benchmarks of Youth

The Unenlightened Will Think of These as "Warning Signs"

This chapter is specifically designed for you readers who are wondering, "Could my children be Trustafarians?" Do not get your hopes up quite yet. Odds are not in your favor. If your children share a bedroom or just really like you a lot, they are not Trustafarians. If you are Hispanic, Native American, or otherwise not particularly white, your children are almost certainly not Trustafarians. Of course, there are plenty of other things they can still achieve in life. They can be astronauts, policemen, and lawyers, but it will not be because of you. Your financial support—love—may be a launch pad, but it is in no way fuel. No one will chide you for having a self-made success as a child, but people will be aware that you did not make your child's success.

Conversely, if your child is a Trustafarian, people will be able to readily calculate your own success as a parent and your net worth. It is the ultimate emblem in passive bragging. Gaudy bling and yapping novelty pets are means to a similar end, but they are heavy! Get an absent Impostafarian son or Fauxlanthropist daughter. People will talk!

Is Your Child a Budding Trustafarian?

While true Trustafarian traits will not manifest until early adulthood, a child will often give telling clues about their future. You can also take some steps to steer your child in the right directions. Here is a breakdown by gender and age group of how promising children transform into partially functioning members of the Trustafari.

YOUNG GIRLS

She is Daddy's Little Girl, but if you even consider not giving into that little shrill voice's demands, you are destroying any chance of her blossoming into a dreaded Trustafarian. She needs to be spoiled.

Television can also help her on her way. Nickelodeon is a wonderful collection of television advertisements aimed at inspiring little girls to want exciting yet safe products to make them the envy of all their friends. It even has award-winning television interspersed!

PBS is like Nickelodeon but free, so it is less impressive to your daughter in the long run. But do not fear if your child is watching it. It has lots of bright colors, so it might not seem like it is free at all. Do not spoil the illusion. Turn off this station when there is a pledge drive, but for your daughter's sake, do not be so present during her watching that she feels like she is not in complete control of her situation. Should a pledge drive come on and she does see it, you will probably be expected to donate, whether to get that smart local station tote or that Mamas and Papas complete DVD collection. For your Trustafarian's sake, you should do it. Let her know the world is hers and she can have whatever she wants. Support public television if you have to.

Here are some signs that your little girl is growing in the Trustafarian direction:

- She will only watch Disney princesses of color.
- Her Barbie has dreadlocks and receives alimony checks from Ken.

- She has left a note for the Tooth Fairy, which reads, "If a tooth gets me ten bucks, how much can I get for a finger? Does it have to be mine?"
- She does not believe in Santa Claus because there is no way all her gifts could fit in a single sleigh.

FIGURE 11.a. *Your donation of $1,000 proves that public television can be premium too, and it wins you a stunning flashlight keychain.*

YOUNG BOYS

Boys will be boys—if you force upon them all that boy stuff. "Boy stuff," though seemingly vague, is actually a very specific term encompassing aggressiveness, sports, not crying, and other sports. Dads, if you teach your boys to be less of a girl than you are, you are repressing all natural Trustafarian instincts. No one, except your enemies, wants you to have a weak son. By this point in the handbook you should know that Trustafarians are not weak. They are powerhouses, like batteries full of energy, just waiting for their circuits to be completed—or more like a battery that rolled under the counter eighteen years ago. They are batteries nonetheless and sources of power and pride. By introducing sports into a young boy's life, you introduce anti-Trustafarian concepts, such as the idea that looking like a loser is somehow shameful or that being in a sweaty pile of men is somehow less than gay.

FIGURE 11.b. *Boy stuff*

Reflect for a moment on the games boys are expected to play as youths. **Red Rover** teaches that the stronger army can just take slaves, simply by calling out their names. **Capture the Flag** teaches boys to focus on the one thing that an opponent most covets and then try to take it away from them. **Tag** leads them to believe that they are so powerful that a single touch can ruin a person. **Tee ball** is an exercise in narcissism, wherein a boy is so good at baseball that he does not even need another player to throw him the ball. **Pretending they were not caught wearing Mommy's heels** may be a challenging game, but having them make an effort to subvert their feminine curiosities just shows them that challenges for the sake of challenges are admirable.

These may seem like just fun and games, but they really attack the budding Trustafarian spirit, which is meant to find its own way—away from its parents.

If you are hoping Junior becomes a Trustafarian, here are some signs he is headed in the right direction:

- Transformers action figures are too lazy to be in disguise.
- He is only good at sports that are on a TV screen and that he can control.
- He enjoys *Sesame Street* for the gritty, urban sensibilities.
- He tries to enroll himself in public school.
- He wants to star in a black film, and play every roll.
- He calls the Haitian women at the Laundromat his "second moms" or "best friends."
- He refuses to cut his hair, and will not even distinguish between the front business section and back party section.

PUBERTY!

When those very first hairs sprout in those rebellious zones, your sweet little brat locks on to a life path that will determine Trustafarian emergence. There is only so much a parent can do. You have given your little girl everything and let her walk all over you. You have told your little boy he is in fact a boy but that doing boy stuff is unessential. Now it is your child's time. You have no choice but to sit back and not watch, either because everything Junior does will be out of your view or because it is too gut wrenching to stomach.

They will be learning about new ideas and rejecting old ones. Full or partial nudism may be practiced in and around the home. In terms of partial nudity, girls may choose to wrap their towels like Dad does with the argument, "Why shouldn't I?"

dreadnut (drĕd´nŭt) n.
Rastafarian: coconut
Trustafarian: a dreadlocked mass of pubic hair

Those Trustafarians destined to be Impostafarians will at this point attempt to get with the Rasta lingo. You will note clever puns like "overstanding" and "downpression" in their daily exchanges. Your home and community will be their Babylon, and you yourself will be a disgrace to humanity. Take pride. Your child is on his/her way!

Fauxlanthropists will find their ways into political discourse. They will set their sights on registering as something you will find offensive, like Democrat or Independent, but you know they will never end up following through and actually voting. It is usually a good idea to play along. You can threaten to take away the country club guest passes if they continue to act up, but there is a good chance they will not be as upset by this as you hoped. It does not matter. If your child is a Trustafarian, the club would not let him/ her in anyway.

Chances are good that this will also be the age where you ask your children to leave home. They have ripened for twelve to fourteen years, and you are ready to empty the nest, send them to boarding school, and set up your second home gym. The freedom your children now have will be the ultimate push toward what they will become. They will make new friends, some of who cannot even be vetted due to years of living off the grid as a homeless person or escapee. Trustafarians are able to find these curious friend types because they frequent the same dumpsters and railroad tracks, seeking supplies, food, and adventure. You may have some parental instinct to protect your Trustafarians. You may want to encourage them to give the homeless money or polite and dismissive apologies instead of friendship. You may want to spend time with them to bask in what they are becoming, but resist. That feral girl who was raised by wolves did not get to be who she is today by having parental involvement, neither will your Trustafarian.

rude boy (rōōd boi) n.

Rastafarian: a juvenile delinquent/youthful badass

Budding Trustafarian: Frederick-Giuseppi Hawthorne, that jerk who makes fun of my Jamaican accent at school

TEENAGE BOYS

Junior is well on his way. As a prepubescent, he avoided the man-making rigmarole. Now he must take on actual rebellion and subversion. Shame seems to dissipate, as taboo subjects, like the hours he spends masturbating, become normal topics of conversation. The video games that, in his younger days, were ways to express faint athleticism are now action-packed ways to relive his real-life driving and street-fighting blunders in vivid detail. The parental instinct in you may want to warn your son about the consequences of driving drunk, but that part of his life has probably already passed and he has smartly moved on to driving under the influence of other things, for which there are not breathalyzer tests.

Here are some signs that your teenage son will be a Trustafarian (and that he hates you):

- He is unpopular at prep school.
- His grades are down, he looks like a hobo, but he is suspiciously popular at prep school.
- He refuses to join the golf team.
- He gets excited when the barrel price for oil falls, as they make excellent drums.
- His clothing looks like wall art from the Santa Fe summerhouse.
- He only wears gold, green, and red, which are particularly ill suited to his pasty complexion.

- He is in love with Denise Huxtable and respects that she was too lazy to show up some seasons/dropped out of Hillman College/phoned in performance for the final episode.
- He has an elaborate plan to show how weed smoking can save lives but also exhibits elaborate lack of follow-through.

TEENAGE GIRLS

Daddy's little princess now has hairy legs and a rack! The girls' path to Trustafarianism generally takes a very different course from their brothers'. At this point there is a complete reversal. They have been given everything. Now they will decide if it is worth it.

Some girls will love it all. In this case, you have—less than ideally—found yourself the parent of a future trophy wife or lady CEO. Alternatively, the Trustafarian girls will resent it all and hate you for spoiling them with such wonderful things. In a rapid change of attitude, they no longer want anything to do with you, but they will be happy to take all of the things you buy them.

Proms and other dances will not give a Trustafarian any excitement, as they will give her peers. Instead they will

FIGURE 11.C. *What she is wearing to prom. Dress: former tablecloth turned into custom dress by Vera Wang, $3,100. Jacket: costume piece left over from Michael Jackson memorial party, $500. Fingerless gloves: made from fingered gloves, made fingerless one night while doing handstand across homemade coal walk, $16.*

simply be viewed as archaic events that have all the hassle of a wedding but lack the compensatory gifts.

Just like at her future weddings, her date will likely be a gay guy or a convict.

Oftentimes, people mistakenly assume that lack of interest in becoming a cheerleader is a benchmark of Trustafarian youth, but this is simply not the case. The days of the banging-hot high school cheerleader exist only as fossils. Years of an inclusive spirit have left the cheering ranks very much filled by the fat and uncoordinated. Hot girls, with absolutely no interest in becoming a cheerleader, drink in the stands with their hot girlfriends. This does not make them Trustafarians.

Actual budding Trustafarians are not so hot and they can be found drinking or smoking up in the parking lot with their one not-hot friend.

Here are some clues that your daughter is on her way to being a full-fledged Trustafarian:

- She refuses to get her eyebrows done or shave.
- She is really excited about getting her period, for metaphorical value.
- She eats dirt to make herself fertile.
- She refuses to join the tennis team.
- She is a total Darlene, not a Becky.
- She cannot wait to tour Bennington's campus.
- She has already outgrown that Rasta beanie from the last Marcus Garvey birthday celebration.

CLUES IN YOUR OWN LIFE

You cannot raise a Trustafarian by trying too hard. This is paramount, and a mistake many parents make, only to wind up with some sort of self-sustained showoff that would rather struggle than take their generously offered easy path. The worst thing you can do is care too much about your kids. Just like prison inmates or the ghosts from Super Mario World, they will only get somewhere when you look away.

How can you gauge your effectiveness in making your kids just as successful as you without them ever having to work themselves? There are some common experiences among Trustafarians' parents. Not all POTs will experience each of these, but similar situations will certainly arise.

- Your drugs are missing and the maid is still miserable.
- You have the munchies after walking by your kid's room.
- When you ask your kid to turn down the hip-hop music, you are loudly corrected that it is *dubtronica* and lectured about its Afro-Caribbean origins.
- Your dealer tells you what a great kid you have.
- At prep school parent-teacher day you are "not what [the teachers] expected," or you notice you are the only parent that was invited.

FIGURE 11.d. *Some of the more impressive items on February's credit card statement.*

- You and your ex both claim it is not your weekend to watch your kid, so it is the other one's fault that What's-its-name is missing.
- When the credit card company calls to ask if you just put 2 million yen for a jet ski on your card, you cannot be sure.

For those of you readers in the proper financial brackets, with a little bit of luck and a little bit of parenting, you may actually find yourself becoming the parent of a Trustafarian, who will be a corporeal testament to your impressive success.

Procreation
LIterally Getting Nasty

> **donkya** (dŏn´k-yə) adj./v.
> *Rastafarian*: don't care, careless
> *Trustafarian*: to have sexual intercourse with the person to whom one is
> speaking "(I am going to donkya!)"

Bloom might not be on the rye, but something is in the air. The all-but-subtle waft of Trustafarian lovestank knows no boundaries. Many hand-books would not expose you to the private grindings of their subject matter, but in this case, you are given an invitation—an opportunity—to watch a veritable car wreck. (Sometimes they do it in moving vehicles. It just adds a little excitement.)

> Trustafarians want what everyone wants—not a soul mate, just a really cool friend to have sex with, possibly long term and maybe exclusively.

From dismissive to obsessive, Trustafarians have trouble with many types of relationships. Trust is often an issue, and they may find themselves sabotaging relationships or potential oral situations by asking themselves too many questions:

- Is this person only after my money?
- How can this person possibly respect me?
- No, really, what does this person see in me?
- I said he was good. What did he lie about?
- I'm not really wearing a condom. What did she lie about?
- Oh my god, for real, what could anyone see in me?

The questions are not easily answered. Asking them risks an undesirable response. Even worse, a partner may re-evaluate what was presumed to be a decent situation. Trustafarians, as in all situations, have their own skewed ways of coping or not coping with problems at hand. Whoopee-making is no different.

Trustafarian Sex Druthers: Nonchalant

This is a very good starting place for Trustafarians. It is also a good stopping point for many who feel that casual is the way to go. Virginity tends to be voided by a rash decision to get it out of the way or a passing, hot piece of "somethin' somethin'." One would not go so far to say that the Trustafarians are entirely for sex, but they are keen to partake in a tolerable shag or polit-ricks (see Trustafarian definition) when available.

> **politricks** (pŏ´lē-trĭks) n.
> *Rastafarian*: the games, deception, and corruption involved in a govern-mental system
> *Trustafarian*: (from *poly*, "many," + *tricks*, "a prostitute's client") an extremely successful evening with multiple sexual episodes

> CLIMAX EVEN HIGHER!
>
> Four out of four Trustafarians agree that ganja improves sex (and anything else).

THE PERFECT MELONS

Trustafarians have gym memberships, but the ones who use them do not do so to keep a healthy body. They use them to keep themselves desirable, and while their nasty bits are steaming on the elliptical, they have a prime piece of sex staple guiding them to hotness. It is the sculpted splendor of the personal trainer.

Trainers train because their life focus has been making themselves look good. It is simply what they know best. The singular motivation for looking good, outside of a media-based career, is easy sex.

The trainers do not have to look far. Trustafarians arrive on their doorstep like a pack of seeds (the kind they would send Mom on Mother's Day because they are cheaper than sending flowers). Just like a farmer growing fruit to make money, the trainers nurture these seeds, making sure they get plenty of water to grow strong and shapely. When harvest time comes, the farmer will evaluate his crop, and after careful selection from his/her supple yield, a few lucky choice melons will be chosen for personal consumption. Trustafarians fall right off the vine, into their trainers' laps.

Ethically, the commencement of a sexual relationship with a client should terminate the parties' working relationship, but this is generally not the case. It is, instead, the termination of a sexual relationship—which generally follows within twelve to thirty-six hours after commencement—that is usually the end of the working relationship. Trainers are able to return their other ripe fruit, and the Trustafarians will simply have to find a new trainer or get fat again.

FAT IS NOT NECESSARILY A TERRIBLE THING.

Only the most active of Trustafarians attend gyms. Candidates for "most active" usually include females and some male Fauxlanthropists. You will often find that Impostafarian and Brohemian males choose to participate in outdoor activities: bike riding, boarding (surf or snow), skateboarding, jogging (often from the scene of a for-fun petty crime), extreme napping, and climbing on things that specifically say to not climb on them. With all those calories burned, there is little need for a gym.

For the Diddlysquatters, and for other *inactives*, chunky is just a part of life for those not blessed with good genes.

A MISMATCHED PAIR

The days of Mom hoping she can find a nice Jewish girl for her son are nearing an end. Once, Rose Fitzgerald Kennedy could not tolerate her daughter Kathleen marrying a Protestant. Her Catholic bias may have been so strong that it prevented Ted Kennedy from really pushing those Northern Ireland peace talks toward the Good Friday Agreement until after her death. Kathleen married in a simpler time, when Rose did not have to worry so much about her daughter marrying a black man, another woman, Eunice, a house, or some sort of cetacean, as has been seen recently. The biggest threat to her family was a vaguely different religion, which, in some parts of the world today, still warrants a stoning. Trustafarians do not visit those countries.

It should be noted that despite her opposition to commingling, Rose F. Kennedy lived to be 104 years old, so she was obviously doing something right.

Modern, wealthy moms need to be prepared for a number of surprises regarding who their children bring home or do in the dressing room at Macy's.

White Trustafarian Female + Black Male

The attraction here often comes from a need to rebel with a *Guess Who's Coming to Dinner* effect, but it is also often a means to revamp one's posse. If incessant shopping with the prep school girls or a fifth on-again-off-again relationship with that Brohemian guy from sixth grade has left a girl feeling stale, appropriating a new crew via dating is a viable and common fix. A complete dumping of former compatriots may seem harsh, but it just may be worth it for the scenery change. It is sort of like a two-hour TV movie from the series *24*, called *24: Redemption*, where Jack Bauer hangs out in Africa for a few hours to liven things up.

A strapping African-American man also connotes promises of protection and safety. Even the most introverted, upper-class, golf-loving black guy is considered by lusting Trustafarians to offer a wealth of street smarts and experiences they will never know firsthand. It is delusion, but for them, it is sexy.

White Trustafarian Male + Female of South/Southeast/East Asian Descent

For some reason, many people are under the impression that this attraction is because of a perceived doting submission of Asian females. It would seem these people are overlooking a few things:

1. There is a ubiquitous pop culture portrayal of a female ninja who can stalk and kill with the grace of a predatory cat. This is considered sexy.
2. It is difficult to forget *Full Metal Jacket* and its "Me so horny. Me love you long time" line. For those who did forget the movie, the 2 Live Crew sampling of the line is ingrained in its place.

3. Business school students (of whom there is often a large concentration of Asian females) party like no others. Sure, it is upsetting to watch such brain cell massacre and degradation, but a turn-on within the community.
4. It comes back to stereotypes about size, and white guys feeling they finally have something to offer.
5. Asian girls seem to really like white guys, for a variety of perceptions and misconceptions involving assertiveness, gumption, and Western ideas of beauty and coolness (standard stuff). White guys, especially Trustafarians, like that they do not have to try too hard.

Velma from *Scooby-Doo*, Psylocke from the *X-Men*, and Miss Scarlett from *Clue* all eventually became Asian to up their crime-solving hotness. Also, though not making the complete racial transition, by the third and final live-action *Teenage Mutant Ninja Turtles* film, April O'Neil found herself wearing feudal Japanese garb.

WAS DAPHNE FROM *SCOOBY-DOO* A TRUSTAFARIAN?

Case for: rich parents, pink headband, only asset for mystery-solving is her wealth, hung out for years after Velma and Fred left to do more grown-up things, vehicle of choice is a big van
Case against: takes good care of hair
Verdict: Trustafarian

A beautiful Indian woman with her MBA, good hygiene, social graces, and overall joie de vivre is not going to find anything tempting about the average Trustafarian, unless her dad left her and her mom alone at some very young age and she has some sort of complex. The Asian + Caucasian pair in the Trustafarian world will be far less glamorous. More common is the white

Trustafarian male matched (for a few hours) with a drunken, chain-smoking Asian American who cannot stay on her skateboard or continually gets her wallet chain snagged on a fence. She likely does not have a job herself, but also probably does not have a trust fund to fall back on. She is intent on finding a beau who does have financial security—either that, or she does not care with whom she knocks boots. At base, the pairing gives her a place to spend the night that is not her parents' home or at least a way to pass time between naps.

> ### KNOW WHAT YOU ARE GETTING INTO OR WHAT IS GETTING INTO YOU
>
> When going home with a Trustafarian, it would be unwise to expect sheets on the bed. Do not get your hopes up. Instead, expect crumbs. It may be gross, but at least you will exfoliate as you writhe around on the bare mattress.

OLD BOOBS

If something does not work the first time, you can usually count on it not working again, but if the sex was good, it might be worth a recall.

Casual sexual adventures begin for Trustafarians in prep school. There is simply too much peer pressure not to do it. The only excuses would be obesity and confirmed, repressed homosexuality. Each guy will date each girl during some point. Dating is foreplay in prep school, though it might take two outings to complete.

Children of poor parents tend to have difficulty finding sex grounds, but for young Trustafarians, whose parents are on vacation, partying, or living elsewhere, there is not much effort in clearing a zone.

These mini-relationships will prove useful in the post-school years of Trustafarian life. This is especially true of the Brohemians, who do not leave their comfort zone and often only associate with their former schoolmates. Where does one call for booty when no new booty is shaking?

The past.

No misstep of teenage years is too great to overcome for a moment of casual adult intimacy.

> **Adult Brohemian:** Hey, Katy (or other name). Sup?
> TRANSLATION: You're single—right?
> **Adult Brohemian:** Any big changes in your life?
> BROHEMIAN TRANSLATION: Are you a lesbian now? Did you get fat or lose a limb?
> **Adult Brohemian:** We should definitely catch up.
> BROHEMIAN TRANSLATION: I'm so going to bone you. And I want you to leave before I go to sleep.

NEW BOOBS

Pressure may come from Mom for her darling daughter to find a doctor to enhance a slighted chest (or to marry). Mom may want her daughter to attract some virile young men, or she may be feeling inadequate about the genes she passed on—especially if her own implants look particularly unnatural next to her daughter. Also, Mom may feel bad that she forced her daughter to drink soymilk all those years when other kids were getting the benefits of growth hormones in regular milk.

The underdeveloped Trustafarians will be hard-pressed to find reason to alter the uninterrupted slant of their thoracic cavities.

Reasons Against Trustafarian Breast Augmentation

- Bras would no longer be optional.
- There may be a loss of nipple sensitivity. Considering how desensitized a Trustafarian already is to life, she prefers to keep the few options she has for stimulation open.

- The enlarged breasts are viewed as a means by which men will objectify them. They would prefer to be subjectively unattractive.
- They are holding out for Keira Knightley (who made one sexy pirate, and passed as a boy while doing it) to successfully usher in the age of unendowed beauty.

To better understand the relationship between the average Trustafarian female and the average woman who seeks to increase the surface area of her chest, examine the following diagram:

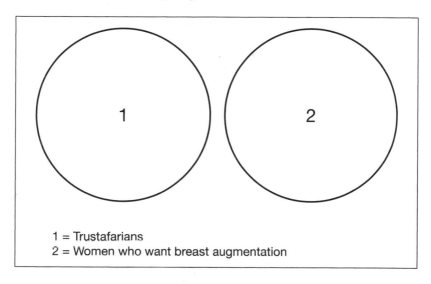

1 = Trustafarians
2 = Women who want breast augmentation

Brohemian males tend to be "boob men," so a Brohemian female may toy with the idea of going under the knife, but for the most part, cons outweigh the pros. There comes a day in most Brohemian males' lives when they realize they just do not meet the standards set by women who spend thousands on their breasts. They will default to what is available and easily within their means, just like always.

Trustafarian Sex Druthers: Extended

While Trustafarians are not prone to making commitments, there are occasions when a combination of factors, such as simplicity, comfort, and new housing, will get them to settle into something a little more official than a one-night (or less) stand.

EASING INTO IT

Sometimes it just happens. Intermittent sexual encounters lead to a toothbrush and combined laundry. Pretty soon, allowing someone to cohabitate between encounters becomes easier than waiting for her/him to make a booty call commute. A Trustafarian may lose interest between the time the call goes out to the time when it is fulfilled, so to avoid that, he/she may choose to keep the booty close.

THE THING THAT DID NOT LEAVE!

This is a variation on easing into it. This plays to an Heirasite's strengths and to the Trustafarian's greatest annoyances. It begins in the late afternoon.

A Trustafarian wakes up and runs his/her arm across the bed, hoping not to graze or overtly touch what spent the night there. After confirming that the Trustafarian is indeed alone in bed, he/she stumbles out of the bedroom to find some Honey Nut Cheerios ...

TRUSTAFARIAN: What the fuck are you doing here?
THE THING: I've been watching On Demand. I'm watching indie horror flicks on fast speed and stopping at the gross killing parts. That's cool—right?
TRUSTAFARIAN: You ate my Honey Nut Cheerios.
THE THING: I'll buy some more, since we both like them.

Six days later the Thing That Did Not Leave still has not left, and the Trustafarian has become inured to his/her presence. The Trustafarian sees continual sex and Honey Nut Cheerios as ultimately beneficial.

> Normally, if someone leaves something at your house, it is a strong hint that they want to see you again. When a Trustafarian does it, they are just being forgetful. Do not embarrass yourself by confusing his/her motivation. Throw that thing away and play dumb if they notice.

MOM LENDS A HAND

In an effort to better her Trustafarian's life situation, an unwitting mom may set her child up with the child of a work associate or rich friend. Trustafarians will tolerate this because they know the joke is ultimately on her. Two scenarios will play out:

Scenario One: Failure

For this example, consider a male Impostafarian. He takes out his date and discovers her to be something he assumed he would read about in *The Devil Wears Prada*. Though he thinks Anne Hathaway is charming, he is ultimately repulsed by this lady's personality. She is kind of hot though, so he stomachs it. She, on the other hand, is just repulsed by his identity (and obviously did not get a copy of this handbook). She orders food that she will not finish and leaves her date with the bill. The evening ends there. Mom failed and the meal is now on her credit card bill.

Scenario Two: Success

For this example, consider a female Diddlysquatter. She meets her date at a Starbucks really close to her apartment and notices that he is averting his eyes. She is pissed off just because she was about to do the same thing. She asks him if he wants to be there. He says, "Dude, no." He is a Brohemian! They decide to throw their hot beverages at a bus and go to Dave & Buster's or some hole of a bar where people still smoke. They both get lost in a fantasy of what it will be like when their parents find out what their date was like. Mom calls the next morning to check in, the now-boyfriend answers, burps, and hangs up. After five minutes of wheezy laughter, he makes out with his now-girlfriend, despite not having brushed his teeth in two days. Mom succeeded—and is now crying.

> SMEGMA
>
> Nature's lubricant: If you have sex with a Trustafarian, it is probably going to show up, rearing an ugly head.

MILFS AND DILFS

Speaking of moms, if a Trustafarian's own birth parent is not helping in the love department, someone else's just might be able to. Cougars and manthers (which you should have heard of by now—or you can at least intuit) are always on the hunt for the energetic, supple, and naive. They offer all the benefits of a parent with added sex and companionship, and unlike a parent, the relationship can be easily terminated at any time. But think about it for a moment. Why would Trustafarians want to end this sort of perfection? Long-term milfing and dilfing can lead to financial freedom from the family, without doing much work at all. Granted, the Trustafarian just enters into a new and potentially rocky phase of dependence, and it can be especially tricky if the MILF/DILF is still legally married. If the relationship between the Trustafarian and the Generation Xer does subside (or explode), parents will likely welcome their precious back into the fold as thanks for getting rid of the old skank.

> ### DID YOU KNOW?
>
> While most people use *skank* to refer to people they do not respect and consider sleazy, it also has another meaning that denotes a particular dance related to reggae music. Trustafarians are unaware of this, but they have never been particularly fazed by any convergence of skanks in their lives before.

FINDING THE PERFECT MEMBER

While they may not have much to Tweet about and their Facebook updates are limited to "bored," "call the cell," and "ia m soo srunk," Trustafarians are still a part of the digital age. Online dating is an arena where they are comfortable enough to dabble.

Facebook (and Those Whom Facebook Crushed)

Facebook is great for Trustafarians; relationship status updates of former prep-schoolmates prove invaluable. Knowing that "Jody Haupt" is now single lets a Trustafarian know when exactly to move in and offer comfort.

Since Facebook was first available to the Ivy League schools where Trustafarians paid little attention, it is the website where nearly all Trustafarian loyalties lie. While most will admit that Tom from MySpace seems like a really cool guy (Do you think he has a Facebook page?), his site did not really establish itself among Trustafarians. That said, older Trustafarians who were exposed to the Internet for the first time as adults and when MySpace ruled the land still maintain active presences there. Often they are able to find each other's profile pages. For the twenty-nine and downward crowd, the site of choice is Facebook.

Remember Friendster? It is still useful. Trustafarians, and others with limited-access pages on other social networking sites, often forget that they once had a thriving easy-access Friendster page with pictures of their shame abounding. It is good for dating research.

Rich People Dating Sites

A quick Google search turns up countless (for people who are perhaps too lazy to count more than ten) web hits for sites offering a rich guy or gal the chance to peruse their databases and find love. Minimal digging traces all of these sites back to a single company in Toronto. Apparently, they know love in the North. How does a Trustafarian know if a site is legitimate?

- He/she is given recommendations from friends who have online dated or read this chapter.
- The company can afford TV commercials that air before midnight.
- He/she does not know, loses some money, but gets to see some X-rated photos of somewhat attractive people: not a total loss.

OkCupid.com

Here is a simple, straightforward website attracting young and sexy people because it is free. No questionable charges will show up on that credit card bill that Mom and Dad get every month.

It is super easy to find a compatible Trustafarian too! Just select your part of the world, a radius, type "Bob Marley" into the interest search box, and click the search button. Within seconds, the hip Trustafarians from the area are listed and dating can begin. Another keyword option for Trustafarians to find other Trustafarians is "unemployed." There is no shame. They own it. They want to be found because of it.

The Millionaire Matchmaker

Anyone with cable and a healthy revulsion of laugh-track plagued network TV (CBS) has watched Millionaire's Club founder Patti Stanger annoy the hell out of them and make them really appreciate their bosses. She takes millionaires, explains to them the reasons why they are losers, and sets them up with hot people (usually girls) with whom they will try to have sex despite her explicit, contrary rules. It seems unlikely to work, but it is indeed a viable option. Stanger has the nation watching to make sure her company is legit, and she wrote a book with some pretty good dating advice. Trustafarians can sign up on her site with a sense of confidence and hopes for love and airtime.

Trustafarian Sex Druthers: Welded Bliss

Well, here is a rarity indeed. Many young girls dream of their wedding days; many young Trustafarian girls want to choke those brides with their veils—and then mess up their ridiculous, stiffly stacked hair.

Why Trustafarians Hate Marriage

- Marriage means a Trustafarian is no longer considered a "kid" at Christmas and will experience a sharp decline in gifts.
- Marriage tells parents that a child is mature, AKA "not in need of their money."
- Marriage will include a painful ceremony in which an unfamiliar rabbi/minister/priest/cantor will summarize the stories of Trustafarian love as best he can remember them from fifteen minutes earlier when he/she was told about them.
- Divorces are expensive; nonmarital breakups just destroy a lamp or two.
- Marriages bring added stress of getting a new cell phone plan (not paid for) or having to go through the trouble of adding a new spouse to the family's plan. That tends to be a bit embarrassing, even for the Trustafarians.

Why Trustafarians Love Marriage

- Wedding gifts!
- Honeymoon vacation!
- Nothing else!

As with the best MILF scenario, a situation may arise in which the Trustafarian continues dependent living away from his/her family. For the change of pace, marriage is generally a good choice.

Trustafarian Sex Druthers: Proliferative

Trustafarians know that sex has a biological purpose: it makes their biology feel really good. If they are not careful, it can also make babies.

A Quick Rundown of Which Trustafarians Want Children	
Impostafarians	No . . . unless the child is black
Fauxlanthropist males	Never
Fauxlanthropist females	Someday, to pour love into
Brohemians	Absolutely not
Diddlysquatters	Shut your ridiculous face!
Heirasite females	Now! Now!
Heirasite males	Force her into it over time

FAMILY PLANNING AND FAMILY WINGING-IT

The women and girls of the Trustafari are all prescribed some sort of oral contraceptive. The idea of a vaginal ring is a bit much as they do not really want to put their fingers in there. The only difficulty with the oral contraceptives is that they need to be taken regularly to work. That is often too much to remember, so sometimes they get pregnant.

Just as with their efficacy in handling STDs, Trustafarians are also adept at handling nature's other little mistakes. Many Trustafarians will skip the doctor's office and just go to the abortion clinic to get a pregnancy test. That way any follow-up can be done in one fell swoop. As a precaution, they may down morning-after pills like Pez.

A Trustafarian will often lament that her favorite children are the ones she did not carry to term.

WHAT DID BABIES EVER DO TO THEM?

Not only do babies feed on breasts and various things left on the floor, they also feed on funding. Trustafarians grow very comfortable living off of a set income, which possibly includes fostering one or more Heirasites. A baby throws them for a financial loop. Not only are they suddenly poorer; they are also suddenly expected to care.

If you have not yet pieced together why an Heirasite would want a child, it is because a child with a Trustafarian ensures their family membership and financial well-being.

Regardless of how they are viewed by society, Trustafarians believe without irony that their lives are too troubled and full of hassles to wish their existence upon anyone else. Choosing not to reproduce is not entirely selfish. It often begins with selfishness that becomes justified by real concern. Even though they may have a really cool name picked out, like "Trench," bringing a baby in this world to suffer like they have just does not seem worth it.

Trustafarians not wanting children is also good for the economy. If there were only more Trustafarians in the world, the wealth of the upper classes would regularly redistribute every few generations. That cycle is, however, interrupted by Aristobrats whose progeny (exclusive of Trustafarian mutations) manage to collect the income of multiple generations and continue to pass it on down the family line.

TRUST FUN! | # Find Your Trustafarian Sexual Identity!

What cultural guide is complete without a sex quiz? Asinine questions and vague mathematics reveal things about yourself that you never knew! Does Jah smile upon your Impostafarian procreation? Are you a Fauxlanthropist in the hemp sack? Find out definitively, once and for all. And then, retake it until you get a result you like. Or be a dick and figure out what your ideal point values would be before taking the quiz and remove all the fun.

1. How far will you go for sex?

- ❑ Painstaking search for a spiritual match (4 POINTS)
- ❑ Find someone with two similar interests (one being sex) (3 POINTS)
- ❑ I'll masturbate if no one is in the bed with me (1 POINT)
- ❑ Booty call from a proven slut (2 POINTS)
- ❑ If I gain financial security, who cares? (0 POINTS)

2. How recently must your sex partner(s) have showered prior to frottage?

- ❑ Same day (2 POINTS)
- ❑ Yesterday (3 POINTS)
- ❑ Smells like yesterday (4 POINTS)
- ❑ Meh (1 POINT)
- ❑ If I gain financial security, who cares? (0 POINTS)

3. Cuddling is _____.

- ❑ Clingy (3 POINTS)
- ❑ You mean I passed out on someone? (1 POINT)
- ❑ I want to! I want to! I want to, but it's too clingy (0 POINTS)

4. My sex toys are _____.

- ❑ Rasta striped or double as bong (4 POINTS)
- ❑ Unsanitary things around the house (1 POINT)

CONTINUED ON NEXT PAGE

❑ Nonexistent or travel vibrator (2 POINTS)
❑ Recycled rubber or purchased from EarthErotics.com (3 POINTS)
❑ Whatever is asked of me (0 POINTS)

5. Position-wise, you _____.

❑ Give the business (2 POINTS)
❑ Get the business (3 POINTS)
❑ Become business partners (4 POINTS)
❑ Race to the bottom (1 POINT)
❑ I've done some things I'm not proud of (0 POINTS)

Now, add up all of your points and see how *you* perform!

0–3 POINTS: **Heirasite**. You are not proud, but you may be successful. Degradation is something you just might learn to get off on.

4–7 POINTS: **Diddlysquatter**. They say streetwalkers and call girls are both just whores, but you know the difference. Your modest success allows you to stay right at home—not that you are a whore, most likely, and not that there is anything wrong with that.

8–12 POINTS: **Brohemian**. Dudes, you're getting more tail than anyone else reading this book. And girl dudes, the guys do talk about you.

13–16 POINTS: **Fauxlanthropist**. Sex for you is as natural as a bear eating a smaller, weaker animal. Undo your hemp belts, hike up your flowing skirts, and go green.

17–19 POINTS: **Impostafarian**. You've called out a deity or some sort of saint's name during sex before, and you'll do it again. You may repress some more wicked things, but at least you feel good about yourself.

CHAPTER 13

What to Do When the Money Runs Out

Not Their Problem . . .
It's Everyone Else's

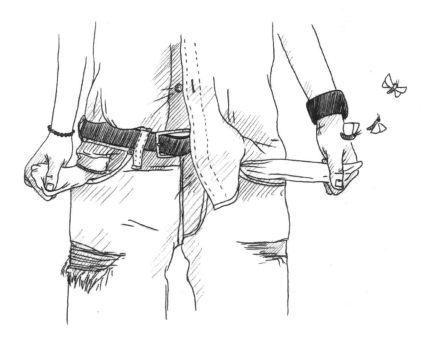

If you have ever been using your laptop and experienced a blackout, you know that your laptop can coast for an hour or two on its battery before becoming entirely catatonic and unable to function. After that, the rest is darkness.

Desktop computers are finished as soon as the power is gone, and Trustafarians are certainly glad they are not that part of this extended metaphor. Desktops are the people who look poor but actually are. The laptops—Trustafarians—at least get some time to figure things out, and they are portable!

Keeping the Power

Their real concern is their power source: Mom or Dad or both of them, whichever is chiefly contributing to the trust. Focus on this is paramount for an aging Trustafarian, and with enough care "What to do when the money runs out?" will never be an issue.

A terminating source of funding can be avoided as long as parental income continues to grow. POTs usually reach their sixties as their children hit their thirties, and by this age, the Trustafarians have figured out a few things. Their self-imposed mandate is that their breadwinner cannot enter into a situation with a fixed income. If they see Dad tiring from his forty years as an entertainment lawyer, they will start to encourage elaborate vacations or other joyous occasions he could take part in if he just continued to take new cases and make more money. In this situation, the Trustafarians will also point out how Mom would be unbearable to live with if Dad had to be home all of the time. Whatever excuse keeps Dad in business keeps the income trickling down.

Remember, Trustafarians are not stupid. Though they may have not paid attention, they have had some of the best educations available on the planet. The result can be ruthless and calculating. If a Trustafarian feels threatened, he/she is going to consider taking action.

OVERRIDDEN WITH GUILT

Parents, prepare for this should you ever decide to suddenly become selfish and keep that money for yourselves—and what a callous move that would be, waiting until your darlings are inalterably moored to your income and then cutting them loose. Parents, how dare you?

It is just like telling your three-time National Dog Show, sponsored by Purina, best-in-show schnauzer that she needs to become feral.

Would you do that? No. You are keeping that dog until you or it dies. Why should your children be any different?

Your Trustafarian understands that you are Dr. Frankenstein and he/she is your monster. If you treat your monster poorly, it is going to haunt you for the rest of your life, and maybe make you chase it to the North Pole.

Parents, love your monsters.

Trustafarians know the unfairness of their situations. Raised having it all, they have to suffer a societal expectation that they should not have any of it. It is the opposite of the American dream, going from everything to nothing. If a POT attempts to impoverish his/her child, the dependent will pounce with a barrage of reproach:

- "Why would you buy me an apartment on my sixteenth birthday, just to make me homeless on my twenty-third?"
- "I guess Mittens can use that money more than I can."
- "It's too bad the only thing I'm good at is being your son, and now you won't even let me do that!"
- "I'm going to kill myself and make you find me."

The exaggerated suicide threats tend to be the most effective because the money POTs give their children to see a high-caliber therapist can be spent on continuing the Trustafarians' status quos.

POORER PARENT RELEGATION

This is a common, clever tactic, and if you are a POT, you should be leery of this being tried on you. At the same time, be honored that you are a party to this splendor. Assume for example's sake, a breadwinning mother, a father who is her assistant, and their Trustafarian daughter.

Mom seems to be getting jealous of her daughter's luxuries and wants to keep that money for herself. She drops not-so-subtle hints like, "Oh, I hear your friend, Madeline, got a job with RBS. I bet that's fun for her."

The Trustafarian takes her cue and begins to hide Dad's things: his glasses, his wedding ring (grabbed while he showered), one of his dress shoes. She offers to set the table for dinner and dulls Dad's steak knife on a stone step out back.

At dinner that evening, Mom and daughter are waiting at the table when dad arrives late in socks because he could not find his shoe. Mom spots the missing ring, and he says he must have left it in the bathroom and goes to look for it. Mom says something along the lines of "You are hopeless" or "I bet it was that new Latino." When he returns again, the daughter shows him a newspaper article about healthy aging, but he cannot read it without his glasses that he "must have misplaced."

He tries to cut his steak but is having a really hard time. Mom starts to see her once-strapping husband as a pathetic old man, and she thinks that he must really need her. While she reflects, across the table, her daughter exclaims, "Crap! I lost my cell phone. Again!" and then, "Dad, I'm just like you."

Mom now thinks this whole family would tank if she were not there to hold it together. Maybe not that night, but soon, she will resolve to do whatever she needs to in order to help her family. She sees that her daughter is not lazy but just the victim of lousy genetics, being cursed with the traits of her feeble old man. Giving the daughter money is now considered instrumental to her survival.

The money will keep trickling in, and all it took was a modicum of deceit and initiative.

Power Failure

There are simply some status upsets that even the most cunning Trustafarian cannot control. At the end of the second millennium's premiering decade, the eyes of financial analysts, bloggers, and regular folks around the world turned to the Trustafarians.

Through the simple monitoring of their changes in living and lifestyle, Trustafarians have become a measure to understand the scope of economic downturn.

Good Economy   **Bad Economy**

Sometimes Mom and Dad just do not control their income. Investments that were once thought to be marginally illegal become simply devastating.

Husbands, who thought aggressive investments would make up for failings in the sack, can no longer afford to pay for disappointed prostitutes. Their wives and ex-wives can no longer afford their payments for surgical Courtney Cox mimicking and lose the interest of college boys everywhere (except their sons, who watch, terrified). Just short of selling shoes for spending cash and cutting their feet open on broken shards of piggy bank, POTs will do something drastic. They will sacrifice their children.

Guilt trips and parent relegation will both be tried, but when parental fund-pulling is not done by choice, those tried-and-true methods have little effect. Here are some alternatives for the flagging Trustafarians:

AFFECTING DENSITY

Most POTS (the ones who can generally remember their children's names) will begin their serious fund pull with typical hinting, but with a directness never before achieved.

> *Get a job, now!*
> *Love,*
> *Mom*

Given that example, you can see that there is room for interpretation. "Now" will always be now. There is never not a now, and jobs can be acquired during a future one. "Job," itself, is vague. "Love" is clearly subject to nonliteral construal.

When the messages of cord cutting come from parents, Trustafarians will be smart enough to find wiggle room in their meaning. Who can really blame them for not understanding?

> *We have to give up your apartment.*
> *Love,*
> *Dad*

Well that is sad indeed, but a Trustafarian will be quick to note there was no time period specified. His/her non-artist's artist's loft can be given up in a year or two.

Your rent is two months late. Give me your front-door key.
Love,
Your Landlord

How could a Trustafarian even begin to admit to understand that one if cornered in person by a landlord? Any verbal response will be "You have me confused with my brother (or sister). That bastard (or that bitch) owes me money too!" Or the Trustafarian can run in fear. He/she can come through a window at some other point. Sacrificing the key, as requested, may be necessary. Luckily, a quick scan of the building and grounds outside will turn up dozens of keys that were previously misplaced by the Trustafarian, who can use one of them to sneak back in.

SHIMMYING BACK UP THE WOMB

When getting back into the apartment is not an option, a Trustafarian may decide to get a job and find a new place, but this is unlikely. Home may be the only option.

Whether or not Mom and Dad choose to delight in the homecoming, the move crushes any delusions of independence a Trustafarian may have had. Bongs must make a return to being continually hidden. Clothes must go back to being worn.

While being terrifically unpleasant and shameful, a return to the old family home (or the new family condo) is not wholly bad. Free food no longer has any middlemen, and laundry no longer has to be dropped off or picked up.

To Crawl Back or Not to Crawl Back	
MOVING HOME	**OUT ON OWN**
don't have a job, pretend working	have a job, working but regularly fired
lose friends upon relocating	lose friends in six to twelve weeks on regular schedule
Mom and Dad pay bills	Mom and Dad pay bills
be reminded why Mom and Dad are hated	hate Mom and Dad, but don't really remember why
be thought of as no-good slacker	be thought of as no-good slacker

The Trustafarian may offer to do chores and projects around the house as a means of employment. The offer will be the extent of the effort. There will be very little follow-through. The goal in moving back in with the parents is that given time, parents will do anything to get the kid back out of the house, including buying the Trustafarian a home of his/her own.

With Trustafarians forced to vacate their trendy neighborhoods, local economies spiral down the crapper. The Trustafarian stool is no longer there to clog the way.

Coffee bars, fusion restaurants, food co-ops, and Laundromats that serve tapas begin closing, and tent cities sprout under their elaborate awnings.

If, during a recession/depression, the Trustafarians manage to stay, due to generous or unwelcoming parents with indissoluble wealth, rents will go up, and the fourteen to twenty-four actual starving artists who actually inhabit the neighborhood will be forced to move back home, or—you know—to the streets.

Without the artists though, the neighborhood will become culturally stagnant and passé. A decade later, when the Trustafarians realize this, they will move out too. Then, the artists can move back. The cycle continues.

Backup Generators

When parents fail to fulfill their financial commitments in the long term, the Trustafarians have some other options besides homecoming and job seeking. The most common is a Trustafarian-type transition: becoming an Heirasite.

If someone's own parents are not working out, one may move on to another's. Girlfriends and boyfriends are great sources of Trustafarian hosts. Of course, the success of this relegation to Heirasitism depends entirely on the social status of the boyfriend or girlfriend.

BEST-CASE SCENARIO

The boyfriend or girlfriend comes from an untouchable, wealthy elite with savings so secure that not even a leeching Trustafarian could waste a notable fraction. With no spending limit, a new Heirasite can return to living comfortably, looking like he/she has nothing.

PROBABLY THE WORST-CASE SCENARIO

The girlfriend or boyfriend is nothing more than an Heirasite, who chose poorly when picking out a mate. Neither one wants to work, though without skills, a job could not be acquired anyway. In ten to fifteen seconds after the legitimate Trustafarian has had his/her funding pulled, the relationship ends, and both begin the search for lucrative love.

BUT IT COULD BE WORSE

The Trustafarian had been involved in a polyamorous triad or quad before Heirasite relegation. The girlfriends and/or boyfriends have been relegated to simple failures. They kidnap the new Heirasite and demand ransom. Having not realized that the new Heirasite's family has no money, the affair ends in passionate murder-suicide-suicide-suicide.

However, if the new Heirasite can come up with a new Trustafarian intimate network where all three or four of them can be involved, death scenarios may be avoided.

EVEN WORSE THAN WORSE THAN THE WORST

The boyfriend or girlfriend is an Heirasite who dumps the new Heirasite and starts bonking the new Heirasite's dad.

It is clear that for safety purposes, a wealthy Trustafarian should always pursue a mate that is not an Heirasite. Too often though, it is the case that a wealthy Trustafarian just does not have the drive to make such a pursuit, and the Heirasites always make it so easy for them to fall, not in love, but into a comfortable relationship. If the money goes away, it is likely that the Heirasite will too, and the Trustafarian is forced to move on or move home.

The previous situations and scenarios are pretty much identical when dealing with nonsexual pairings, such as those with friends or the guys who sleep on Trustafarians' couches.

A Special Note to Trustafarians Who Have Lost Funding

Dear Trustafarians,

You did not realize that the word Trustafarian *applied to you until it was too late. Mom picked the new sofa set over giving you free housing, and now you have come to this handbook for answers. The Trust Fun sections in this book are not for people who want to get a good chuckle at your expense, they are for* you *and for anyone who wishes to enter the world of Trustafarians again or for the very first time.*

You may be feeling very alone right now, and it is true: you are. The number of Trustafarians who actually lose their money is nowhere near as large as you would like it to be.

But still, you—Trustafarians—are survivors. Get your asses out of The Game of Life *and get them back onto the laps of people much better suited to playing. Times may be dark, but do not give up. Do not give up until you are part of a zombielike horde of Heirasites that has begun to consume the last surviving rich person. As long as people have money— and a handful of people always will—fight to get it, but do not go too far out of your way. You are above that sort of vigorous effort. Embrace your inner Heirasite and be a selfish Robin Hood, until you have enough to not have to try any more.*

Yours now,
The Trustafarian Handbook

Dreads courtesy of not showering

$9.95 Goodwill baja

Bus schedule

All of his belongings

$1 (he *will* bend down to get)

Last taste of açai until the economy's fixed

TRUST FUN! | ## Comforting a Fallen Trust Friend

Stipendiary losses leave Trustafarians feeling despondent and in need of a true friend. Here is how to show a Trustafarian that you care.

STEP 1: Send a text message saying, "heard what happened sorry."
STEP 2: Do not respond to future texts from your Trustafarian, and do not answer his/her calls.

The money is gone, so why should you care? If you find your incessant humanity to be a problem, you can of course reach out, but beware the pitfalls:

- If your Trustafarian spends a few nights on your couch, the word *few* will take on a whole new meaning.
- If you enjoy having a stocked fridge, you will come to enjoy it more due to its increasing rarity.
- If your Trustafarian finds you are not using some of the items around your place, he/she may sell them for weed or for beer or for take-out or for a masseuse or for a pretty fighter kite.

Current Forever

The smart Trustafarians, who have successfully avoided misfortune, will enter their forties without having sacrificed their titles. As of now, not a lot is known about Trustafarians after this point in their lives.

Decades of societal pressure for them to do something with their lives may cause them to take actual jobs. To avoid scrutiny, others may go into hiding and wait for their parents to die. All the Trustafarian types have unique options available to them, but only time will tell which they choose.

OLDER IMPOSTAFARIANS

If they are still Impostafarians come middle age, these men and women of the Trustafari have a relatively rich religious life, which will inform their futures. Relocation is an option for adult success. Since they can afford them, homes in Jamaica and Ethiopia make great options. In both countries, Afrocentric culture abounds, and the Impostafarians can be active in the local religious kinship.

Visa limitations may make it necessary for them to fly out of their adopted homes every few months, but they can probably afford the travel.

Another viable option is for an Impostafarian to begin a reclusive pot farm, nestled safely somewhere in a red state, where no one would think to look for him/her. Smoking up and dealing to local teens makes for a quiet and sedate adult life. Also, when stoned, the constellations in the open night sky could actually start to look like things, like bears. After a few weeks, they will not fear the sky bears.

OLDER FAUXLANTHROPISTS

If he/she was smart, one of the charities that the Fauxlanthropist started is one that will give money to aging Trustafarians as their money dwindles. Another option for the artistically inclined (regardless of talent) is living in their art galleries, sleeping in a back room, and painting during the day while no one comes in to see their art. They can always say they have an apartment somewhere else for legal reasons and to abide by zoning laws, but this can of course be a lie.

Another option for members of this green-leaning Trustafarian troop is living on a self-sufficient farm. It is earthy, and it does not matter if money ever runs out. Though, of course, the Fauxlanthropists will be regularly accused of not pulling their own weight and will be told to clean a toilet. Then, someone just gets paid to clean the toilet for them. Life could not be simpler or more fulfilling, though it would be nice if they could get Internet out on the collective.

Nicole Buffett

Warren Buffett has a bit of a back-and-forth with Bill Gates when it comes to taking on the title of World's Richest Man. He is often said to live below his means, not flaunting his wealth. If he only did not make that money himself, he would be a Trustafarian.

Nicole is his granddaughter—well, his son Peter married this lady, who had this daughter who is Nicole, and then Peter and the lady got divorced.

Nicole is an artist.

She gained exposure through the 2006 documentary *The One Percent*, which followed the financially free children of wealth and one of them was Buffett. She also appeared on *The Oprah Winfrey Show*, sporting her dreadlocks pulled back nicely and neatly for her TV appearance.

She does not have a trust fund, and after her media stint, Warren Buffett apparently sent her a nice letter explaining that she was in no way part of his family. Still, a child of the wealthy, with dreadlocks and an art career . . . you behold a Trustafarian.

She is working her last name, getting noticed, even though she gets no funding from her mother's ex-husband's dad. She is in a limbo between the omigod rich and the pitiful poor, which is not a position any Trustafarian envies. With no natural niche to fall into, she is doing the best she can, even though that cash would seriously help her out.

OLDER BROHEMIANS

Bros that stay together, get gray together, and decay together.

You might think at first that Fauxlanthropists are most likely to wind up living in a commune, but needs to aggregate funds in midlife years may cause a Brohemian to share a queen-size mattress with seven of his/her best friends. The pressure for these Trustafarians to find work or the semblance of a career is probably greater than with any other Trustafarian type. Impostafarians, Fauxlanthropists, and Heirasites have much more palpable goals, and the Diddlysquatters—well—they are just immune to most pressure.

Working at a video game store is an excellent choice for work, as there is not a ton to do. A Brohemian can steal video games, and customers never expect great customer service anyway. Other viable careers include bartending, stripping, filming weddings, law enforcement, volunteer coordination, human resources, and restaurant ownership.

Guys who choose to roll out of the Bro bed may find themselves saddled with a very successful wife, who for reasons she hates, is hopelessly attracted to assholes. Lady Brohemians will likely find themselves married to ugly CEOs, for whom they were the best available trophy wives.

OLDER DIDDLYSQUATTERS

After forty, Diddlysquatters are still probably sitting in that same studio apartment next to the McDonald's where they still order delivery. They probably have not left in fourteen years. They are napping and smiling on the inside.

OLDER SUCCESSFUL HEIRASITES.

Against all odds their dreams came true. A female Heirasite will likely be the proud mother of a screwed-up—beyond repair—kid and the happy wife of a generous old man. A male Heirasite will likely be a happy, homemaking husband with addictions to expensive cable packages, *All My*

Children, painkillers, and online shopping. Another option for midlife is being a divorcée or a divorced man. Most who marry will do so with a hasty elopement, so that no soon-to-be POT in-laws have time to chime in about prenuptial agreements. Legality can get messy though, especially if a spouse's parents control his/her funds, so staying married is a safe way to go.

After forty, Heirasites may also be found sitting in prison, convicted of killing their spouses, awaiting release and a glorious money shower.

In whatever way they achieve their success, they probably used this handbook to help—which will not hold up in court. Do not try. Killing is a legal no-no.

FIGURE 13.a. *Heirasite success! You know you have been rooting for them all along.*

The Trustafarian Manifesto

This would be a final Trust Fun! activity were it not such a serious exercise. For all of you who have completed this handbook and decided to claim the path of Trustafarians as your own, this is your declaration of dependence. Remember each of these points as you undertake your difficult journey. To help, stand in front of a mirror each day and recite them, averting your eyes until you finally see a Trustafarian before you.

The Trustafarian Manifesto

1. Breeding will be carried out by exception only.

2. High-society functions will not be attended.

3. Anything financial will always be handled by another party.

4. Loft apartments will be achieved.

5. Parent = Necessary Evil.

6. Follow-through will not be expected; new projects will always be started.

7. The fight to legalize marijuana will be observed, stoned.

8. Naptime will be observed.

9. One will always ask, "How would a Kennedy get away with this?"

10. Employment will be staved off by any means possible.

11. Eight hours of labor a day is unreasonable.

12. Less than eleven hours of sleep a day is unreasonable.

13. Breadwinners must not be allowed to cease breadwinning.

14. Hair will not conform.

15. Failure will be tolerated.

After you finish reciting these, take a long, deep breath, sigh, and go back to sleep.

Acknowledgments

For her stories, excitement, and insight, especially during the early phases of writing this book, thanks to Ellie Schiffer. Also thanks to the talented Yamil Comrie for his Rastafarian insights. Huge thank-you to Brendan O'Neill for this opportunity, and many thanks to Brooklyn, the East Village, and Western Massachusetts for years of information on the subject of Trustafarians.

Further gratitude to Joshua Scott, Anne Kirkpatrick, Joshua Taylor, Sergio Espriella, Sebastien Kuo, John Swartz, John Zuarino, Mindy Vieira, Stacey and Rob, Ian Boissonnault, and Hanna Homan.

And, of course, thanks to John and Karen Griffin for housing and food during much of this writing process.

Index